THE
POWER
OF TIME

About the Author

Pauline Edward (Quebec, Canada) is an astrologer-numerologist and professional speaker. She is the founder of A Time for Success, a consulting business specializing in Trends, Cycles, and Lifestyle Planning, offering counseling, coaching, and workshops for individuals and businesses worldwide. A Time for Success is the proud winner of a prestigious West Island of Montreal Chamber of Commerce Accolades award for excellence in business practice.

True to her 14/5 Life Path, Pauline's journey has been enriched by a broad range of experiences from the mundane to the mystical. When not working with clients, she can be found indulging her passions for writing, renovating her home, gardening, working on her cha-cha, or hosting dinners with family and friends. Learn more about Pauline's services, events, workshops, and publications on her website: www.paulineedward.com.

THE
POWER
OF TIME

◆ ◆ ◆ ◆ ◆

Understanding the Cycles of
Your Life's Path

◆ ◆ ◆

Pauline Edward

Llewellyn Publications
Woodbury, Minnesota

First Edition
Second Printing, 2008

Book design and layout by Joanna Willis
Cover design by Gavin Dayton Duffy
Cover image © Photodisc

Llewellyn is a registered trademark of Llewellyn Worldwide, Ltd.

Library of Congress Cataloging-in-Publication Data
Edward, Pauline, 1954–
    The power of time : understanding the cycles of your life's path / Pauline Edward.—1st ed.
        p. cm.
    Includes bibliographical references (p.   ).
    ISBN 978-0-7387-1149-2
    1. Numerology. I. Title.
    BF1623.P9E39 2007
    133.3'35—dc22
                                                                              2007026017

Llewellyn Worldwide does not participate in, endorse, or have any authority or responsibility concerning private business transactions between our authors and the public.

    All mail addressed to the author is forwarded but the publisher cannot, unless specifically instructed by the author, give out an address or phone number.

    Any Internet references contained in this work are current at publication time, but the publisher cannot guarantee that a specific location will continue to be maintained. Please refer to the publisher's website for links to authors' websites and other sources.

Llewellyn Publications
A Division of Llewellyn Worldwide, Ltd.
2143 Wooddale Drive, Dept. 978-0-7387-1149-2
Woodbury, MN 55125-2989, U.S.A.
www.llewellyn.com

Printed in the United States of America

In loving memory
Robert H. Edward

Contents

Acknowledgments

This book was written to answer the diverse questions asked by my clients, friends, and family, who, in many ways, have given me more than I have given them. With each encounter, I have been blessed with tremendous opportunities for learning and growth, and for this I will always be thankful.

I am particularly grateful to my parents, without whose support I could never have pursued my destiny. Because of them, through my work with astrology and numerology, hundreds of people have found their unique life paths and are now living richer and fuller lives. A special thank-you to Veronica Schami for a superb final round of edits; to Michele Lanteigne and Epp Luik for proofreading the manuscript; and to Bob Winters, who, while making certain I always had a computer to work with, never once doubted in my abilities.

Many thanks to the Llewellyn team for their vision and confidence in my ability to put this book together, in particular to acquisitions editor Lisa Finander for reminding me to keep things simple, Gavin Dayton Duffy for a great cover, Joanna Willis for her patience with the numerous graphics, publicist Marissa Pederson for her enthusiasm and energy, and editor Karl Anderson for his patience and thoroughness.

A final note of acknowledgment goes to two numerologists whose works contributed significantly to my understanding of this wonderful system of knowledge, Hans Decoz and the late Matthew Goodwin.

About This Book

The Power of Time is not a complete textbook of numerology. Instead, it introduces the basic set of numbers derived from the date of birth. In a complete study of numerology, the numbers from the Birth Name, current name, nicknames, and numbers linking the Birth Date and name numbers would be used. Although a fascinating study in its complete form, many people would feel overwhelmed if faced with the prospect of analyzing and interpreting twenty to thirty number values.

This book was written for those who, like my clients, spend valuable time planning and goal setting, both professionally and personally, and want to know more about the natural cycles at work in their lives. Most of these people have careers as well as family responsibilities, and simply don't have the time or the inclination to undertake the years of study normally required for the mastery of numerology.

The Power of Time focuses on the numbers derived from the date of birth not only because they are simple to calculate and easy to learn, but also because they clearly reveal the path of your life, like a road map you might use for direction on a long journey. A large part of this book will be devoted to the Personal Year number, probably the single most powerful tool for planning and goal setting. Exercises have been included throughout to help you easily integrate and apply the information. As you discover the natural cycles and trends at work through your numbers, much of the pressure and anxiety that normally exists when steering the ship of your life into uncharted waters will disappear.

Who Should Read This Book?

This book is for those who would not normally read a traditional numerology book. The approach is practical and hands-on, very easy for the person with a hectic lifestyle to use. Given the powerful system of knowledge contained in the numbers, anyone who wants a clearer sense of direction should read this book. This book is for you if:

- You are intimidated by numbers and would appreciate a simplified introduction to numerology.

- You have absolutely no knowledge of numerology.

- You have an interest, but not the time for an extensive study.

- You have some knowledge or experience with numerology and would like to know more.

- You wouldn't be caught dead consulting a numerologist, but your curiosity got the better of you.

- You'll try anything once.

- Someone you respect recommended this book, and now your curiosity is piqued.

- You don't believe in anything that can't be scientifically proven, so you've decided to prove that numbers don't work, although unconsciously, a part of you secretly hopes to find some measure of truth.

But mostly, this book is for you if:

- You need to clarify your life purpose and get back on track.

- You want to have a better sense of control.

- You want to set and achieve exciting new goals for yourself or your business.

- You have some decisions to make and don't know where to turn.

- You have a busy schedule and want to make the best use of your time.

- You want to be certain to take advantage of your opportunities at the right time.

- You seek a better understanding of the forces at work in the lives of the people close to you.

- You are at a crossroads and ready to make a fresh new start.

By reading this book, you will:

- Gain a deeper understanding of your life purpose.

- Learn how to sort out what is important to you from what is not.

- Learn how to focus on your needs and opportunities given your trends.

- Learn how to make your action plans even more effective.

- Identify and learn how to deal with potential obstacles.

- Gain the knowledge and confidence you need to achieve your goals.

Mostly, you will feel much more in tune with your natural cycles and will experience increased confidence, greater success, and an overall sense of satisfaction.

WARNING: This book will change the way you plan for your future!

Introduction

In 1994, I had the fortune of taking a course in the ancient craft of numerology with a wonderful lady. This experience came at just the right time, for the knowledge I gained helped clarify why my life was in such turmoil, why things weren't going the way I wanted them to, and, more importantly, what I could do to set myself on a healthier course for the future. Having studied and practiced astrology for nearly three decades, I already had a good sense of my life purpose, but somehow circumstances had piled up and I felt as though I had temporarily lost my way. Numerology provided me with a fresh new angle on my situation, shedding light on a state of affairs that at the time seemed insurmountable, giving me not only the hope, but also the knowledge and understanding I needed to get back on track.

Since integrating numerology into my practice, I have found that many of my clients are quite eager to learn about the cycles at work in their lives. Numerology is much easier to learn and use than astrology; an exact time of birth is not required, and calculations are limited to simple sums and subtractions. This book was written for those who, like my clients, would like to incorporate some of the basic principles of numerology to improve their planning and goal setting.

The Best-Laid Plans . . .

It's not uncommon to find ourselves participating in conversations that center around how hectic the pace of life has become. We share how overwhelmed we feel, how we struggle to find—never mind maintain—a balance between our personal and professional lives. By the looks of it, this trend isn't likely to abate any time soon! Despite our concerns, it would appear that we are far more resilient and adaptable than we might have imagined, for the more curves get thrown at us, the more we appear to cope. Nonetheless, judging by the growing number of people suffering from anxiety, sleeplessness, burnouts, divorce, and stress-related illnesses and disorders, it would appear that our coping mechanisms leave much to be desired.

> *Always plan ahead. It wasn't raining when Noah built the ark.*
> RICHARD C. CUSHING

But help abounds! Bookstore shelves stacked high and deep promise solutions for all aspects of our lives from physical, mental, emotional, relational, and spiritual to financial. We're reading about work-life wellness, balance, making better choices, creating effective habits, living with purpose, effective goal setting, love and relationships, the importance of visualization, the relationship between job satisfaction and health, manifesting with intention, longevity, productivity . . . the list is endless. We're applying all manner of clever plans, systems, approaches, and methods. Compared to even just twenty years ago, we have an astounding, perhaps overwhelming, abundance of resources available to us today.

To top it all off, we seem to be living in an ever-expanding cult of self-accountability. We are encouraged to become responsible for the outcome of our lives. Our success, we are taught, is the result of not only our talents and abilities, but also of our thought patterns, our belief systems, and our ability to focus on our goals. The pressure mounts. We are taught to visualize with intention, to create and affect the future we wish to experience. Our future lies in our hands. If we aren't reaching our goals, we must be doing something wrong, we aren't working hard enough, or we don't believe in our goals or ourselves enough. For many people, gone are the days of blaming parents, schooling, the economy, politics, and society for their defects and woes. *Your* decisions, *your* actions, *your* power, *your* results, *your* responsibility, *your* fault. Faced with the heavy burden of responsibility for their own success, some people never leave the starting gate, fearful of possible failure once they commit themselves to entering the race.

Suppose you've been applying yourself diligently at uncovering your life purpose and developing healthy new habits. You've hired a coach. You have a support team. You've read the books and produced what you think is a dynamite, fail-proof plan. You've worked on your attitude; you're motivated. You diligently write your affirmations and practice visualizing your intentions. You're focused. Yet, despite the best-laid plans of man and mentor, unforeseen circumstances arise and trends change, getting in the way of your progress and eventually diminishing your feelings of satisfaction. Your confidence begins to falter. You wonder where you went wrong. You can't seem to get it right. Why are you not making the progress you expected in the time frame you had so painstakingly determined?

Here's a good question: have you ever stopped long enough to ask yourself whether or not you were applying the correct methods at the correct time? Not in terms of market trends, seasons, or any other external factor, but the right time for you, in terms of your own natural cycles. Would you expect to harvest tomatoes from a seedling planted in the middle of a January frost? Of course not. No matter how good a gardener you are, it just wouldn't work. Rather than arbitrarily establishing deadlines and target dates for attaining personal, business, and financial goals with no valid sense of whether or not the timing is right, imagine if you could establish a real timeline, one that made sense and was in tune with your personal seasons. Imagine the power and effectiveness of such a working tool! By reading this book, you will become aware of some very powerful natural cycles at work in your life through the set of numbers that are derived from your date of birth. What better test of a system of knowledge than to experience it directly in your life?

On Predicting the Future

Some people take offense at the idea that events can in some way be predetermined or that they can be forecasted. They fear that if they consult astrology or numerology, they will be influenced and may lose the precious freedom to make their own choices. *Why consult the stars?* they ask. *I know where I'm going, what more will it give me? I don't believe in destiny; I'd rather determine my own future. I don't want anyone to influence my decisions.* These are indeed legitimate questions and objections.

While I was searching for an interesting and effective way to respond to these objections, an avid golfer pointed out that the game of golf was a metaphor for life. Intrigued,

I did a little digging and found a way to explain how I use astrology and numerology. My research led me to discover that golf is a complex and fascinating sport. It has rules, dress codes, social protocol, business etiquette, environmental issues (to spray or not to spray), sex (balls and sweet spots), and Zen-like attributes (stillness, focus, presence). No wonder so many people get hooked! Most golf courses, I learned, provide a card with a map. There are also pins marking the locations of the holes. So, while you keep your eye on the ball, you have a general idea of the terrain you must cover and a clear picture of where you are going.

Now I ask you, does the fact that you have consulted the map predict how well or how poorly you will play? Because you are aware of the layout of the course and have focused on the pins, has the outcome of your game been predetermined? Is your freedom to play your best game diminished? The answer to all these questions is a resounding no. The fact of the matter is that consulting the map helps you focus your attention on your game, lets you concentrate on your swing, and most likely improves your chances of a favorable outcome.

Everyone will agree that in the end, practice, skill, training, and mindset will determine the outcome of your game, and not the map or the pins. Maps are there to indicate direction, terrain, potential obstacles, and distance. They enable you to make an effective plan, determine time and measures, and choose the route that is most suitable to your needs, abilities, and goals. Would you play golf without a map or pins? You could, but with no idea of the layout of the course, it might take you a very long time to complete eighteen holes. Now I ask, why live your life without a map?

You don't have a map? Actually, you do. As we will show, the numbers derived from your date of birth provide you with the map and the pins of the course of your life. They reveal information about the layout of your journey, indicating the bumps, obstacles, twists and turns, opportunities, timings, trends, and tendencies. You remain free to play out your game as you choose. A good map simply helps you play your best game.

There is in fact a vast difference between being foretold the details of your future and having a practical sense of trends to come. It's much like when you consult the weather network for the upcoming weekend forecast. The weatherman checks his weather maps and patterns and interprets the data for you in a way that you can understand. A low-pressure system will bring warmer temperatures and rain; a cold front might indicate a sunny day. We take this information and plan our activities accordingly. Yet at no point does the weatherman actually *tell* you or determine *what* you will do on that rainy or sunny day. He simply gives you the information from the data that he has been trained to read. You are left to make decisions about what you will or will not do on that particular day. You also accept that there is nothing you *can* do about the forecasted weather system. You can choose *what* you will do, but you can't change the weather pattern to one that is more suited to your desires or needs.

A similar situation applies when you consult an astrologer or numerologist, who is in many ways like the weatherman describing upcoming climates and weather systems. Only in this case, she is describing your personal weather patterns. You remain free to decide what you will do given your trends, but there is little you can do about the trends themselves. In this book, you will learn to identify your upcoming trends with sufficient accuracy and detail to enable you to make better choices based on your personal climate. You will in effect become the captain of the ship of your life rather than a passive participant subject to the tides of the future.

The Numbers Used in This Book

In this book, we will study the numbers derived from the Birth Date, including the Life Path, Birth Day, Personal Year, Month, and Day numbers, Pinnacles and Challenges, and Life Path Periods. This set of numbers effectively maps out the entire course of your life, facilitating short-term and long-term planning and goal setting.

In addition to descriptions of the cycles and their trends, you will find exercises along with tips and tricks for making the most of your personal cycles. Sometimes when you're in the thick of it, it can be difficult to be objective and to come up with creative solutions. This book will provide you with a framework, and some helpful and even fun ideas for making your journey all the more productive and certainly more enjoyable.

The Life Path and Birth Day numbers are part of the core numbers that also include the numbers derived from your name, which are not included in this work. By completing the "My Experience of the Numbers" exercise in chapter 1, you will have a good indication of which of the numbers are among your core numbers.

A complete study of the numbers and related cycles is not only beyond the scope of this book, but is also not its intended purpose. If you should experience a period that seems particularly unclear or challenging, I encourage you to consult a professional astrologer or numerologist. An objective perspective on what appears to be a complex or difficult situation can help you obtain the clarity you need to get back on track.

How to Use This Book

You are no doubt eager to learn what the numbers hold in store for you. This book has been organized in such a way as to provide you with maximum benefits in the shortest amount of time. By completing a few preliminary steps, you'll be ready to design a super plan for your future.

1. Chapter 1 introduces the numbers. Complete the exercise "My Experience of the Numbers." By acquainting yourself with the language of the numbers, it will be easier for you to interpret their influence in your life.

2. Next, sharpen your pencils. In chapter 2, we begin with the calculation of the Life Path number. Complete the exercise "Where Am I Now?"

3. Chapter 3 introduces the important Personal Year number. You are no doubt eager to move ahead and find out what your year holds for you. Take the time to complete the "Key Life Sectors" and "My Personal History" exercises. They will improve your ability to plan effectively and provide you with deeper insights as to how the numbers work in your life.

4. Chapters 4 to 12 provide an in-depth description of each of the nine Personal Years. Complete the workshop associated with your current Personal Year. Use this information to set goals that are appropriate for you, based on your personal cycles.

5. For a more global picture of your life journey, complete the tables and exercises in chapter 13.

6. In chapter 14, you will put all your numbers together in a handy reference table. This will give you a clearer perspective on where you are and where you are going.

7. Understandably, once you have completed the basic calculations, you will want to jump ahead to the chapter that pertains to your current Personal Year. By all means do so, but for added benefits, afterward do read the sections on all the Personal Years. With a complete picture of the 9-Year cycle, you will make more effective plans, and maybe even manage to work in an extended vacation or sabbatical in your next 9 Personal Year.

Most of all, remember to have fun with it! Planning and goal setting need not be tedious chores. Within the context of your current situation, use your creativity and imagination to take full advantage of the energies at work in your life.

ONE

Introducing the Numbers

NUMBERS ARE EVERYWHERE

There's no hiding from numbers. We deal with them on a daily basis, from the moment we wake up in the morning and strain an eye to read the digital clock until we switch channels on the remote to catch the late-evening news on our preferred local station. The study of numbers has captivated us for millennia, and can be found in every discipline, including mathematics and science, art and music, the occult, and most religious and spiritual systems. Today, a growing number of entrepreneurs, managers, and other highly educated people are using numerology to plan their lives. Foolish and superstitious people you might say? What if numerology really *can* give you the inside edge?

How does numerology work? The fact is that we don't know exactly how it works, only that hundreds of years of study and observation show that it does. Note that apples fell from trees long before Newton discovered the law of gravity, and numerology will continue to work until science discovers more of the mysteries of the universe. In the meantime, why not use this amazing body of knowledge to your advantage?

Numbers are everywhere. Some people have a favorite number, a lucky number, or even an unlucky number; others are completely intimidated by numbers. Almost everyone has secret numbers such as PINs, codes, and passwords. My client Ken became very excited when I pointed out the age of 57 as an important turning point in his charts. For many years, the number 57 has been a recurring theme. Whenever 57 appears on a bill, address, or telephone number, for example, he sees significance in that moment. The age of 57, I explained, was the most likely age for his retirement rather than the age of 55, as he had originally planned, since 57 corresponds to the end of one of his long-term numerology cycles. The end of a cycle often manifests as the end of a period of activity, such as a job, relationship, career, or project. Months later, Ken informed me that revised financial projections and the state of the economy had caused him to readjust his plans. He is now right on track for reaching his retirement goals at the age of 57, the beginning of a new phase of his journey.

Tomatoes Won't Grow in the Snow

Like many entrepreneurs, Ken is intuitive. Without knowing anything about numerology, he had tapped into an important turning point in his cycles. In his case, it had shown up in seemingly incidental ways. Many people have a sense of their timings without being aware of their numerology cycles. It's not uncommon for clients to express surprise when I point out upcoming turning points from their charts. "I've always had a feeling that such and such would happen when I reached forty-two," they might say.

For example, you might have sensed, intuitively, at some key point in your life that it was time to do something in particular. Maybe you followed a hunch and introduced yourself to a certain person who later provided important opportunities for you, or you applied for the position you wanted *just at the right time*, or you signed up for a particular course in college that *just happened to turn your life around*. Some people don't listen to their inner voice. You know these people. They are the ones always complaining about their rotten luck. They are the ones who say, "I should have done it when the timing was right, but I didn't listen to myself."

If you had been aware of your numerology cycles, you would not have found anything unusual about your decision and its accidental result. Numerology clearly shows your trends and their most likely outcomes. By the same token, given the force of the cycles and trends at work in our lives, no matter how hard you may wish for something, if it's not the right time, it simply is *not* the right time. Those are the times when, no matter how hard you try, things just don't seem to work. You won't grow tomatoes if you plant them in the middle of a January frost. Yet, although you can't cheat your cycles, you can work with them and take advantage of the opportunities they present.

There Is a Time for Everything, and a Season for Every Activity Under Heaven. . . .

From birth to death we are subjected to the influences of countless cycles—some internal, others external—from our biological cycles to the four seasons, to the cycles of economics, finance, real estate, and politics. We are exposed to trends in the arts, movies, marketing, and fashion, as well as health, diet, self-help, and spirituality. Yet, despite all these common influences, how is it that your best friend is falling in love and you're not? Or your colleague got the promotion and you didn't? Your coworker broke the monthly sales target and you had your worst month ever? Your neighbor is vacationing in the Bahamas while you have to stay home to deal with a broken water main?

Although we all experience many of the same cycles and seasons, no one expects our lives to follow the exact same course. Each of us has a unique set of rhythms and timings, the nature of which, as you will soon discover, is revealed by the numbers derived from your date of birth. Once you become familiar with these numbers, the patterns of your life will take on a whole new meaning. You will have a better understanding of why things happened the way they did, how you got yourself into your current situation, and what to expect in the years to come. The cycles of numerology will help clarify your direction and strengthen your purpose. You will see that, in effect, there is . . .

> a time to plant and a time to uproot . . .
> a time to weep and a time to laugh,
> a time to mourn and a time to dance . . .
> a time to search and a time to give up,
> a time to keep and a time to throw away . . .
> a time to be silent and a time to speak. . . .[1]

The Hidden Knowledge Behind Your Birth Date

Numerology is essentially the practice of assigning numeric values to dates as well as to the names of people, places, and objects. This book focuses on revealing the world of knowledge that is hidden in the numbers that are derived from your date of birth. These numbers constitute the road map of your life, portraying its twists and turns, obstacles and challenges, adventures and opportunities.

---

1. Eccles. 3:1–7 (The Family Keepsake Bible, New International Version).

Numbers are fun and easy to work with, and the techniques for using them are straightforward. Your numbers act as signposts, indicating not only the start and end of specific periods, but also the climate of those periods. Some years are more favorable for growth and expansion. At other times, you would do better by being receptive and flexible rather than active and adventurous. Certain years are great for career advancement, while others are best for dealing with family issues. Being aware of your personal climate during a particular year, you can focus on those activities that are appropriate given the nature of that period.

As you will discover, knowledge of your numbers can be of tremendous value, saving time and eliminating much of the guesswork and frustration that might arise when planning a trip without a road map. By using the unique set of numbers derived from your date of birth, you can effectively map out the entire course of your journey. Your Birth Date alone will reveal the important numbers and cycles at work in your life including:

The Life Path Number

The Life Path is the most important of the numbers derived from the date of birth. It reflects the characteristics and traits of the lessons, challenges, and opportunities you will encounter and is in a way the main road map for your journey. Familiarity with this number alone can be very helpful when making important decisions, especially with respect to career and general direction. Your Life Path number will clarify why certain career choices are more appropriate than others.

The Birth Day Number

The number of the day you were born describes specific attributes at your disposal and provides important indicators as to the type of career that would be most suited to your nature. It also reflects the nature of the important middle years of life, the second Life Path Period. This number will help you refine your choices when used in conjunction with the Life Path number.

The 9-Year Epicycle

This very important cycle, including the Personal Year, Personal Month, and Personal Day numbers, describes the short- to medium-term periods encountered along the way and gives you the clearest picture of where you have been, where you are, and where you are going. This book will focus mainly on this cycle, in particular the Personal Year, as it provides the most comprehensive system of knowledge for planning. The Personal Year is the number you will work most closely with when choosing activities and setting goals on an annual basis as it describes in great depth your climate for the year, its challenges and obstacles, as well as opportunities for growth, learning, and success.

The Life Path Periods

The three broad periods of life—the early developmental years of childhood, the productive middle years of adulthood, and the final period of integration—act as a backdrop to the shorter cycles. While of far less significant influence than the Life Path and Personal Year numbers, they do indicate unique tendencies in effect during these periods. The first Life Path Period in particular can be very helpful in identifying and unblocking potential that has been buried since childhood.

Pinnacles and Challenges

These cycles describe trends, opportunities, and learning lessons along the way. They give the overall climate of specific periods and, when combined with the Life Path and other numbers active at a given time, will help you to address and deal with circumstances and also to take full advantage of the opportunities at hand.

Introducing the Numbers

Each number carries a unique energy signature and is defined by a specific body of attributes. When a number is associated with a person's life journey, as is the case with the Life Path number, it tells a story about the nature of that journey. As you will soon learn, the number 5 speaks of change, adventure, and diversity of experience, whereas the number 4 indicates stability, order, and a structured lifestyle.

With an understanding of the numbers at work in your life, you can make choices that are appropriate for your particular energy signature. You would not expect a person with a 5 influence to be content sitting behind a desk in a routine nine-to-five job—in fact, he would most likely grow resentful of his limiting circumstances and probably quit. The 4 person, on the other hand, normally happy with a structured and ordered lifestyle, would feel insecure if he happened to lose that same routine job and were suddenly faced with material uncertainty and change. The 4 person needs routine, while the 5 person seeks change.

How to Work with the Numbers

In the practice of numerology, numbers are always reduced to a single digit, so that you will work mostly with the numbers 1 through 9. For a birthday on the eighteenth of December, the number 18 would be reduced by adding the 1 and the 8, for a result of 9. December, the twelfth month, would be represented by the number 3, the result of adding 1 and 2. In working with Birth Dates, it is important to perform the calculations in the order specified throughout the book, or else important information derived from certain special numbers could be lost. Always reduce the numbers for the day, month, and year before completing the sum.

The Master Numbers

There are two exceptions when applying the rule of reduction: the numbers 11 and 22 are never reduced. For a November birthday, the eleventh month, you would use the number 11. For a birthday on November 22, use 11 and 22, rather than 2 (1 + 1) and 4 (2 + 2). The numbers 11 and 22 are called Master numbers. They tend to vibrate at a higher rate than their single digit counterparts, and may indicate a larger potential than the 2 and the 4. About 25 percent of the charts in my files contain a number 11 among the core numbers (the main numbers from the Birth Date and the Birth Name), and 15 percent contain a 22. In this book, you will find references to the Master numbers written in the following manner: 11/2, and 22/4.

The Karmic Debt Numbers

The numbers 13, 14, 16, and 19, called the Karmic Debt numbers, constitute another set of special numbers. They are generally written as 13/4, 14/5, 16/7, and 19/1. Although reduced to single digits in all calculations—13 reduces to 4, 14 reduces to 5, 16 reduces to 7, and 19 reduces to 1—the double-digit numbers are taken into consideration in the final analysis. For example, a Life Path with a sum of 13 is reduced to 4, but the number 13 would be considered as being *behind* the number 4. The result can be expressed as either "four from thirteen" or "thirteen four." The Karmic Debt numbers represent additional lessons that need to be learned before the energy of the number can be expressed in a completely positive and productive manner. Over one-third of the charts in my files contain one Karmic Debt number among the core numbers, one-quarter contain two, and fewer contain three or four.

The Language of Numbers

As you begin to work with the numbers, you will discover that they have a language of their own. Each number is like an archetype, manifesting an energy that expresses itself in a distinctive set of characteristics. These characteristics can vary from positive and constructive to negative or even destructive. Each person has a unique relationship (ranging from positive to negative) with each of the numbers, even with those that do not figure prominently in their core numbers. In fact, the lack or absence of a number is a relationship of sorts, which, as we will soon see, is an important consideration. Take the time to become familiar with the traits of each number. This will make it easier for you to apply the knowledge of the numbers to your particular circumstances.

As you read the keywords beginning on page 8, notice how the numbers are like a complete system, with attributes and traits evolving and flowing from one to the next, like a stream widening its flow as it merges with other streams, growing into a large river, ending its journey where it joins the sea. So too the human experience builds and grows more complex as we move from the singleness of the 1 to the tension and duality of the 2. The merging of two then explodes with creative force in the 3. In order to not be engulfed in a chaotic surge of creativity, the 3 adds a 1 for stability. So we find order and structure in the 4, only to be stimulated once again into movement and change by the addition of a 1 to the 4 for the destabilizing energy of the 5. The 6 represents even more complex energies at work, comprised of three pairs of 2s, or two pairs of 3, generating a sense of responsibility toward others with a need for balance and harmony. The 7 adds an additional element of specialness with a lone 1 added to the responsible 6. The 8 manifests the ultimate worldly and material accomplishment with its pair of 4s or four 2s. The 9, the result of the addition of a 1 to the 8, brings us to a point of completion and wholeness, leading inevitably to dissolution, in preparation for a new beginning. What was meant to be has become; what is yet to be has not yet been defined. And the cycle begins anew. You will see this process of birth, growth, and completion at work in your life in the 9-Year Epicycle and on a yearly basis in the Personal Year numbers.

Following is a list of keywords that reflect the character of each of the numbers 1 through 9, as well as those of the Master numbers 11 and 22, and the Karmic Debt numbers 13, 14, 16, and 19. Familiarize yourself with the basic traits of each number. Refer to this list after calculating your numbers in the chapters that follow. By using these keywords, it will be easy for you to obtain plausible interpretations for given periods of your life.

The goal of this work is to give you the tools that will facilitate improved self-understanding as well as stimulate your insights and creativity during the planning stages of your activities. Being in the right place at the right time means that you know yourself and also have a keen sense of timing, two essential ingredients for achieving personal success. A basic understanding of your numbers will give you that ability.

Numbers Keywords

1

New beginnings, initiative, renewal, individuality, energy, rebirth, creativity, inventiveness, adventure, courage, assertiveness, will, determination, pride, leadership, entrepreneurship, inspiration, autonomy, self-reliance, independence, innovation, enterprise, opening up to new horizons, reorientation, focus on self, drive, authority, executive ability, progressiveness, breaking from the past, establishing new patterns, creating new habits, setting new plans into motion.

Negative expression: selfishness, insensitivity, impulsiveness, having an overbearing personality, dictatorial behavior, stubbornness, bossiness, self-centeredness, laziness, apathy, greed, narrow-mindedness, impatience, low self-esteem, shyness, retiring personality, self-deprecation, insecurity, cowardliness, helplessness, meekness, weak will.

2

Relationships, cooperation, sensitivity, mediation, receptivity, reaction, conciliation, collaboration, consideration for others, teamwork, focus on the needs of others, partnership, reliance on the goodwill of others, service, flexibility, love, affection, sincerity, adaptability, attentiveness, kindness, hospitality, graciousness, support, sympathy, tact, tolerance, devotion, loyalty.

Negative expression: dependency, indecision, shyness, neediness, oversensitivity, apathy, snobbery, rudeness, obstinacy, fear, taking things personally, unclear boundaries with others, second-guessing oneself, codependency, lack of self-reliance, moodiness, negativity, weak will.

3

Communications, creativity, optimism, heightened mental activity, sociability, fun, community involvement, inspiration, romance, entertainment, enjoyment of life, having a good time, self-expression, drama, relaxation, artistic ability, the lighter side of life, luck, enthusiasm, affection, imagination, kindness, love, loquaciousness, charm and wit, originality, hospitality, style, image, humor, youthful spirit.

Negative expression: disorganization, superficiality, gossip, empty promises, wastefulness, indiscretion, childishness, tactlessness, unkindness, pettiness, envy, pessimism, procrastination, overdramatization, vanity, inability to concentrate, lack of attention, meanness, unpleasantness, coarseness, criticism, negativity, depression, moodiness, callousness, immaturity.

4

Focus, order, structure, foundations, organization, work, determination, fortitude, practicality, service, purpose, health, money, home, routine, family, fundamentals, honesty, loyalty, day-to-day matters, paying attention to details, matters requiring dedication, discipline, persistence and patience, trustworthiness, reliability, dependability, responsibility, management, rigorousness, thoroughness, traditional values, business, steadfastness, commitment.

Negative expression: getting stuck in a rut, inflexibility, perfectionism, negative attitude, feelings of limitation, fear, monotony, resentment, selfishness, meanness, resistance, envy, dogmatism, narrow-mindedness, laziness, impracticality, wastefulness, stubbornness, rudeness, callousness, stupidity, obstinancy. Lack of purpose, focus, and direction.

5

Freedom, liberation, diversity, release from the drudgery of day-to-day responsibilities, expansion, movement, growth, creativity, versatility, exploration of new horizons, lifting of restrictions, pushing away boundaries, travel, adventure, experimentation, new experiences, originality, progressiveness, creativity, inspiration, daring, resourcefulness, jack of all trades, sociability, change and unexpected events.

Negative expression: impatience, choosing freedom over responsibility, dullness, fear of change, being stuck in a rut, erratic or inconsistent behavior, seeking change for its own sake, instability, risk taking, irresponsibility, undependability, unreliability, lack of dedication and focus, failure to learn from experience, inflexibility. Overindulgence in sex, food, alcohol, and other sensual pleasures.

6

Responsibility, family, love, focusing on the needs of others, accountability to oneself and to others, healing, service, stability, understanding, devotion, justice, balance, creativity, artistic ability, seeking harmony in the environment and in relationships, protectiveness, romance, helpfulness, trustworthiness, dedication, giving, generosity, peacefulness. Being helpful to family members, coworkers, and friends.

Negative expression: meddling, blurred boundaries with others, inability to say no, resentment of responsibilities, overinvolvement in the affairs of others, pride, worry, anxiety, jealousy, cynicism, small-mindedness, unkindness, pettiness, selfishness, meanness, insensitivity, vindictiveness, manipulation, smothering, possessiveness, insecurity, pessimism, hopeless victim or victimizer, negativity, excessive idealism.

7

Analysis, introspection, reflection, thinking, isolation, time-out, meditation, need for solitude, understanding, deepening the learning experience, specialization, study, focus, clarity, silence, subtlety, being informed, creativity, need for space and privacy, spiritual quest, studiousness, profundity, looking beneath the surface of all things, seeking the meaning of life, reason and rationality, scientific mind, problem-solving ability.

Negative expression: pessimism, secrecy, confusion, criticism, feelings of superiority over others, plotting, suspicion, cheating, negativity, doubt, deceit, selfishness, antisocial behavior, skepticism, fear, simple-mindedness, dullness, self-consciousness, childishness, insincerity, superficiality, thoughtlessness, imprudence, foolhardiness, narrow-mindedness, stupidity, dishonesty.

8

Power, realization of goals, achievement, authority, the peak of accomplishment, maximum results, confidence, rewards, recognition, money, drive, ambition, success, management ability, organizational skills, leadership, boldness, responsibility, making things happen, realism, practicality, dependability, loyalty, strong personality, organization, entrepreneurship, vision, efficiency, good judgment, directness, honesty, straightforwardness, focus and dedication.

Negative expression: insensitivity, dogmatism, greed, domineering or overbearing personality, intolerance, poor judgment, materialism, excessive ambition, obstinancy, unrealistic expectations, arrogance, selfishness, shyness, weak will, irresponsibility, stubbornness, acquisitiveness, procrastination. Lack of focus, vision, and direction.

9

Humanitarian endeavors, philanthropy, the big picture, charity, selflessness, empathy, compassion, completion, endings, social consciousness, community-mindedness, broad vision, imagination, creativity, the arts, sensitivity, perfectionism, releasing the past, preparing for the future, passion, drama, consideration, sympathy, inspiration, sociability, love, readiness to be of service, helpfulness, generosity, idealism, sense of fairness and justice.

Negative expression: self-indulgence, selfishness, resentment, criticism, negativity, lack of gratitude, coarseness, insensitivity, projection, blame, excessive idealism, emotionalism, aimlessness, drifting, fickleness, unrealistic expectations, discouragement, outrageous goals, inability to share emotions, unkindness, apathy, short-sightedness, lack of vision and imagination.

The Master Numbers

The Master numbers 11 and 22 are given special consideration, and are the only numbers not reduced to a single digit when calculating results. Their energy is often not manifested to its full positive potential until later in life, when a certain level of self-awareness and maturity has been developed. Sometimes, the positive potential is never fully expressed. People with a Master number among either their name or Birth Date numbers often have a deep feeling of special purpose in life. It takes courage and positive support from family and the environment to manifest this potential.

11

Like an intensified or highly sensitive number 2, the 11 is the number of subtle relationships, sometimes acting as a link between this world and others beyond. People with 11s are usually highly intuitive. It confers sensitivity, idealism, progressiveness, imagination, vision, mysticism, uniqueness, a sense of special purpose or specialness, and tends to be emotional and often dramatic. Sometimes it gives a heightened sixth sense that can be used in a helping profession.

Negative expression: excessive sensitivity to people and to the environment, self-absorption, fanaticism, irresponsibility, lack of realism and good judgment, impracticality, superiority complex, obstinancy, narrow-mindedness, difficulty finding a place in the world.

22

Like a more expansive and ambitious number 4, the number 22 is the Master Builder, seeking great and tangible accomplishment. It gives big ideas, a sense of personal power, and tends to be highly ambitious. Its energy is not easily harnessed in the early years of life, and even later, unless a conscious effort is made at bringing out its full potential, it is not often fully developed. The 22 is inventive, inspiring, enterprising, strong, resourceful, generous, giving, productive, creative, progressive, and a leader and great problem solver.

Negative expression: scheming, feelings of inferiority, resentment of responsibilities, vengeful nature, lack of accomplishment, wasting of talents, a sense of worthlessness, frustration, anger, lack of direction and focus, inability to accomplish goals, selfishness, stubbornness, wastefulness.

The Karmic Debt Numbers

The Karmic Debt numbers 13, 14, 16, and 19 denote areas that require special attention, challenging situations, and personality traits that can only be corrected through conscious application and learning. Ignoring these traits will usually delay or hinder your progress. Until their lessons are learned and the energy is expressed positively and effectively, these numbers tend to manifest negatively.

Each Karmic Debt number carries the traits of the single digit to which it is reduced, but these traits are usually expressed in an exaggerated or distorted manner. With self-awareness and conscious application to learning its lessons, the negative energy of a Karmic Debt number can be transmuted into the positive expression of the number and often into a far superior manifestation of its single digit counterpart. It is more strongly felt in the Life Path than in the other numbers derived from the Birth Date.

If your birthday is the 13th, 14th, 16th, or 19th of any month, you have a Karmic Debt among your core numbers. Look for Karmic Debts behind (i.e., before the final reduction to a single digit) the Life Path, Personal Month, Personal Day, Pinnacles, and Life Path Period numbers. Karmic Debts provide additional information about the challenges you are likely to face.

Note that it is easy for beginner students of numerology to panic and become overly concerned when encountering a Karmic Debt number at work in their cycles. As we have seen, Karmic Debt numbers are quite common. Simply consider it as a more advanced lesson requiring added attention and effort, which can, once mastered, lead to superior results. Many highly successful individuals have Karmic Debts among their numbers, as indicated below.

13/4

The lesson that needs to be learned with the 13 Karmic Debt is appreciation for hard work. The 13 can indicate selfishness (1) and a tendency for laziness and the avoidance of, or resentment toward, the restrictions and limitations of life (3). Persons marked by the 13/4 tend toward negative, rigid, and dogmatic thinking and can be heard whining and complaining about how difficult life is, or how they wish they could just quit their jobs, or whatever situations they feel are restrictive. They may have an underlying feeling that their lives are unfairly difficult, that there are always obstacles to be overcome, and that they never seem to get a break. Luck is definitely not on their side. Developing an appreciation for and a positive attitude toward hard work, service, order, diligence, and attention to detail releases the tremendous power inherent in the 4, resulting in a potential for substantial material gain and personal accomplishment. (13/4 Life Paths: Betty Ford, Oprah Winfrey, Helen Schucman, Donald Trump, Frank Sinatra, Elton John.)

14/5

The 14 Karmic Debt represents a lesson in moderation and balance. The individual struggles with a desire for freedom (1), and sometimes will seek it at any cost, even abandoning stability and security (4). The 14/5 often manifests as a tendency for excessive sensory stimulation, such as abuse of food, sex, alcohol, or drugs. Individuals marked by the 14/5 can be highly erratic, impulsive, and inconsistent, and tend to avoid commitment for fear of loss of personal freedom. They experience much change in their lives, and often leave a trail of incomplete life experiences. Failing to learn from these experiences, they repeat the same errors over and over again. They need to learn to be flexible and open to new opportunities while remaining focused on their goals. Through the conscious application of moderation and a willingness to make long-term commitments, the number 14/5 can be transformed to manifest tremendous creative versatility. (14/5 Life Paths: Lee Iacocca, Steve Martin, Dennis Quaid, Steven Spielberg, Liv Tyler, Coretta Scott King.)

16/7

The 16 Karmic Debt brings a lesson of depth and integrity of experience. This Karmic Debt marks the struggle between selfish desires (1) and the necessity for service and love of others (6). Individuals marked by the 16/7 are often isolated and introspective, withdrawing from the very interaction they need to heal their inherent selfishness. They avoid open interaction for fear of being criticized, hurt, or rejected. They may have difficulty finding satisfactory relationships. Overly analytical, they can be highly critical of others, negative, and may even feel superior to others in some ways, usually intellectually. Their tendency to seek answers deep within gives them the advantage of being able to learn some of the deeper lessons of life. Those with the 16/7 often undergo several major life-transforming experiences throughout their lives. By learning humility, adopting a positive attitude, and overcoming their relationship fears, 16/7 individuals can access their great potential for analysis through learning and expanding their understanding of the human condition. (16/7 Life Paths: Dr. Phil McGraw, Jerry Seinfeld, Emma Thompson, Lady Diana Spencer, Marilyn Monroe, Joe Cocker.)

19/1

The 19 Karmic Debt represents a lesson in tolerance and balanced self-love. Individuals marked by the 19/1 can be overly willful, stubborn, and too independent. In the 19, self-centered interests (1) are extended into all ambitions (9) or submerged by fear and lack of courage. The result is a potential for an attitude of intolerance and abuse of power toward others. If the individual has self-confidence issues, the 19 can manifest as an inability to act and pursue desires and ambitions. Individuals marked by the 19/1 may have a sense of entitlement and believe that the world revolves around them. They need to learn love, tolerance, and acceptance of others. Once the negative aspects of the number have been consciously mastered and its lessons learned, the 19 indicates tremendous potential for enviable success and happiness in all areas of life. (19/1 Life Paths: Tom Cruise, Ernest Hemingway, James Arness, George Clooney, Walt Disney, Joe Pesci, Sally Field.)

If Time Is Linear, Then Why Does It Suddenly Stop?

Time is perceived as being linear. Looking back, most people can trace the significant and not-so-significant events of their lives from early childhood to adulthood: the first day of school, a trip with the family, a move, family breakup, a first kiss, death of a grandparent, graduation day, a first job, marriage, birth of a child, divorce. . . .

For as long as I can remember, the future has presented itself in my mind in a linear fashion too, like a timeline unfolding straight ahead, with markers for months, seasons, special events like holidays, business events, family gatherings, and year ends. There is bright sunshine and budding greenery for springtime; bold flowers and more sunshine for summer; the hues of deep orange, reds, and yellows and darkening skies mark autumn; and cold gray and white for winter. (I guess you wouldn't be surprised if I told you I also dream in color.)

However, I do take these images simply as symbols of the general trends ahead, acting as a backdrop for planning and setting goals for the future. I place only required and scheduled events on this timeline, leaving the details to unfold as they arise. Preferring to rely on inner guidance for most of my decisions, I've always shied away from setting too many specifics on my future timeline, lest I prevent an important lesson or opportunity from presenting itself. Yet, the basic framework of a timeline frees me to plan more effectively, to schedule events and set goals for appropriate times, within realistic time frames, and to comfortably deal with situations and circumstances as they occur. This allows me to live mostly on a day-to-day basis without worrying about the future.

Wanting to make a point about planning for the future, I conducted a survey among family, friends, and clients. The question was as follows: when you look ahead into the future, how do events present themselves? I specified that I didn't want to know what their goals were, but rather how they saw their future unfolding. Did they see a road, a path, a calendar, or a line? To my great astonishment, I learned that although the past is generally perceived as being linear, very few people perceive their future in a linear fashion. Many see events in clumps around them, one week at a time, things that have to get done; others see the future as a sort of clock, or dial, with the future going around and sometimes spiraling upward. One friend's future presents itself as a ladder, something she must climb. Only one person described her future as appearing on a line ahead of her.

A few people admitted to preferring not to look into the future for fear of what they might encounter, kind of like closing your eyes when you know that something bad is about to happen. They feel that they have enough to deal with in the present moment. Some who had experienced sales and motivational training were more apt to have specific goals, generally seen as hanging *out there* somewhere in the great beyond, commonly described as a *big blue sky*. However, given the absence of a timeline, they couldn't say exactly when they expected to reach these goals, or how they planned on reaching them. Others were content to not have specific goals and gave little thought to what might arise in the future. Yet all had wishes for the future: a happy retirement, health, a nice big home, a special person they wanted to meet, or the big career move they deeply desired. What they didn't have was the road map for getting there.

One of the powerful features of numerology is that it describes the cycles at work in our lives, cycles of varying length, from daily, monthly, and yearly to cycles that last many years. As you have seen, each number corresponds to a unique set of traits. The number 3 relates to communications, creativity, and social activity, while the number 4 reflects order, structure, and organization. When I incorporate my numerology cycles into my timeline for the future, the picture becomes even more interesting. For any given year, there is a corresponding number that gives unique information about the trends for that year. This is called the Personal Year number. Instructions for calculating your Personal Year number will be found in chapter 3. If I engage in activities that reflect the nature of this trend, I am more likely to experience success than if I ignore it and choose to involve myself in an activity that is contrary to its nature.

Say that the number that corresponds to the current year is a 3. That means that my timeline for the year is colored by the energy of the number 3. I would know that in order to take full advantage of the energies available to me at this time, I should focus my attention on developing my social network, tapping into my creativity, writing, and maybe even making a little time for fun and entertaining activities. The year that follows will have a 4 influence, and should be a year of focus, structure, and organization, basically a work year. If I have taken time out to relax and enjoy myself in the 3

Personal Year, I will be refreshed and renewed, ready to buckle down to work in the 4 year. Also, any creative projects begun in the 3 year are likely to be structured and given form in the 4 year. Knowing my Personal Year cycles, I can focus on what needs to be done rather than worry about what I should do or whether or not I'm doing the right thing.

You may find this strange, but although I have practiced astrology and numerology for nearly forty years, I actually don't care to know my future, at least not in all its details. What would be the purpose of living if I knew everything in advance? I enjoy uncovering my potential and discovering opportunities for using my talents and abilities. Then why use numerology? There is a vast difference between knowing the details of your future and having a general sense of upcoming trends. One will take away your sense of discovery and adventure, while the other will strengthen your sense of purpose and direction. Imagine embarking on a voyage to a faraway destination without a road map. It would probably appear like a daunting, even impossible challenge. Knowledge of your numbers is similar to using a road map. The map remains your guideline; how you experience the journey is a combination of the choices you will make along the way, as well as factors beyond your control such as the weather, traffic, and events.

Your numbers will tell you the following:

- Where you are headed
- What types of experiences you are likely to encounter
- How best to take advantage of your opportunities

Exercise: My Experience of the Numbers

As a first step in defining your life journey, it is essential that you have intimate knowledge of the one making the journey—*you*. Self-knowledge is an essential ingredient to successful planning and decision making. You may already be familiar with your personality profile through consultation with a professional astrologer or numerologist or other tools such as Myers-Briggs profiles. For those who are seeking to deepen their self-understanding, the following exercise has been included to help set the stage for the planning exercises in later chapters. Keep in mind that the better you know yourself, the more likely you are to make choices that best suit your true needs, desires, values, talents, and abilities.

As mentioned in the introduction, this book does not cover the numbers derived from your name, only the numbers from your Birth Date. As the name numbers provide important information about your character, values, talents, and abilities, this exercise has been included in order to complete your self-portrait and help you gain a better understanding of your relationship with the numbers. The more self-aware you are, the more effective you will be in applying the knowledge relating to the numbers at work in your life. If, for example, you were about to encounter a period where the number 3 was highly active, and you were aware that you were lacking in the positive attributes of this number, such as social skills, creativity, and a positive attitude, you could spend more time integrating its qualities into your life. The 3 period would then be much more rewarding.

We all, over time, slide from one end of the scale to the other, sometimes expressing the more positive attributes, at other times the less favorable characteristics of a number's energy. As we grow in self-awareness and take responsibility for our decisions, responses, and actions, we slide to the positive side. To manifest the less positive qualities of a number, one only has to exaggerate or distort one of its basic traits. During periods of excessive stress, we can slide toward the less desirable expression of our numbers. Overall, the average person will express mostly the positive traits most of the time.

Also keep in mind that not all of the positive attributes of a number can be expressed fully at first try. Because a person has an 8 Life Path, it does not necessarily follow that he will automatically be comfortable and effective in a function as leader and director. A certain amount of experience and maturity is required in order to fully manifest the positive traits of this number. Nor will a person with a 6 Life Path automatically find perfect love just because it is in the nature of the number to seek and attract harmonious and loving relationships. I know of many 6 Life Path individuals who have enjoyed long stretches of single life, while there are many 5 Life Path individuals, a number usually associated with change and a strong need for freedom, who are happily married for the duration of their lives to the same partner. There are therefore a variety of possible expressions for each number, and what we make of our numbers is very much up to our choice.

The important thing is to be sufficiently aware of your experience of the energies of each of the numbers so that when one is activated in your life, you will better know how to respond. If you recognize that you have an excess of the number 1 energy, a 2 Personal Year might prove to be particularly challenging in the area of your personal relationships since it requires that you be flexible, receptive, and aware of the needs of others. On the other hand, this same overabundance of 1 energy can become super-excited and exaggerated in a 1 Personal Year, causing you to be more independent and creative, but also perhaps more aggressive or willful than normal.

Another point to keep in mind is that you may experience the numbers differently at various times of your life. The serious and private temperament of the 7 will serve someone well in a career that requires research and analysis without causing too many problems of solitude, whereas that same 7 might have been a difficult energy to deal with if, as a child, the person was surrounded by outgoing personality types.

In the following paragraphs, pay special attention to the descriptions that push your buttons. Okay, some of the character traits aren't very flattering, but everyone has a dark side. While we may occasionally swing away from the ideal, like the pendulum, we always return to the middle in search of balance. Note that each person experiences the full range of energies manifested by the numbers. You may find that you resonate with two or three in particular. You may also resonate more with certain numbers at different periods of your life. When you apply the numerological cycles to your personal timeline, you may be startled by the relevance of your observations. Be honest with yourself—nobody's watching. Be matter-of-fact, rather than critical, and have fun with it.

My Experience of the Number 1

Balanced Expression of 1 Energy

If your relationship with the energy of the number 1 is well balanced, then you enjoy a healthy dose of self-reliance, autonomy, and independence. You like to direct the flow of your life on your own terms. You are original, creative, intuitive, and generally active, and have excellent leadership, executive, and administrative potential. You like to start projects, and then move on to something new. Your energy and drive inspire others to higher levels of performance.

Deficient or Underexpressed 1 Energy

A lack of 1s may manifest as a lack of assertiveness and even laziness. You lack motivation and rely on others to get things done. You avoid doing many of the things you dream of doing because they just seem like too much work. Sometimes you will give in to the demands of others because you are afraid to stand up for yourself. You lack firmness and assertiveness, and have little faith in your judgment or in your abilities.

Overabundance of 1 Energy

You tend to be dominant and overly aggressive, and will do almost anything to get your way. The world centers on you; you like to be center stage. Your selfishness will cause rifts in your relationships as you trample over the feelings of others. You are willful, stubborn, bossy, and egotistical.

How I Rate Myself:

Lack   Balanced   Excess

My Experience of the Number 2

Balanced Expression of 2 Energy

The balanced 2 energy manifests as an awareness for the concerns of others and an ability, and probably a preference for, working with others in a group situation or partnership. Your main qualities include tact, adaptability, cooperation, modesty, receptivity, diplomacy, and sensitivity to the needs of others. You can handle delicate situations with grace, equanimity, and distinction. You have excellent social and people skills, yet are modest and can be a bit shy. You are an attentive, supportive, and affectionate lover and seek harmony in your relationships.

Deficient or Underexpressed 2 Energy

You come on like a bull in a china shop, insensitive to the needs of others. You lack tact, diplomacy, and sensitivity and can say things that are injurious to others without being aware of it. You prefer to do things by yourself, even going out of your way to avoid asking for help. You resent those circumstances when you must work as a team. You get impatient, especially when it is necessary to wait for someone else before you can do what you want to do.

Overabundance of 2 Energy

You are overly sensitive to the needs and opinions of others, sometimes going overboard in your eagerness to please and find love. You then feel resentment when people do not reciprocate with gratitude and service. You can be shy and fearful. In fact, your definition of who you are is based on what others say about you. You tend to take things too personally. Your need for love, affection, and attention seems to be endless, causing problems in your personal relationships. You seek the ideal relationship, a fantasy that lies only in your mind.

How I Rate Myself:

Lack   Balanced   Excess

My Experience of the Number 3

Balanced Expression of 3 Energy

When well balanced, the number 3 shows a generous talent for self-expression. Often the 3 energy manifests in an artistic field. You enjoy sharing ideas and fun times with others. You are considered to be the entertainer of your group, the life of the party, always one to enjoy a good laugh and to have a good time. Your artistic and creative talents may remain dormant. You are sociable, witty, happy-go-lucky, joyful, gracious, and charming. People easily gravitate toward you.

Deficient or Underexpressed 3 Energy

You are very self-critical, stopping yourself from ever expressing your inner inspiration. You suffer from acute "perfectionitis," and you will find something wrong with your performance no matter what. Overly serious and fearful of criticism, often with a pessimistic outlook, it is difficult for you to simply enjoy yourself and appreciate what you have.

Overabundance of 3 Energy

You tend to take things much too lightly, adopting a cavalier attitude, especially when the finger gets pointed in your direction. You are disorganized, trite, and superficial, and spend far too much time gossiping. You are wasteful and scatter your energy in questionable activities. Having difficulty seeing into the depth of situations, you can miss the point.

How I Rate Myself:

Lack   Balanced   Excess

My Experience of the Number 4

Balanced Expression of 4 Energy

You are conscientious, an excellent organizer, and very hard working. You are the quintessential worker bee, appreciating order, routine, and stability in all things. You are practical, conservative, patient, down-to-earth, and approach new circumstances with caution and reason. You are an excellent planner and can tend to the many details and intricacies of a project. You are responsible, loyal, honest, conscientious, and reliable. Family, home, and financial security are important to your well-being.

Deficient or Underexpressed 4 Energy

You may have difficulty finding your place in the material world. You function more with intuition than with order, method, and discipline. Your ideals are lofty; you are a free spirit and prefer to not have to deal with the drudgery and details of day-to-day routine. You are impractical and disorganized, dislike limitations of all kinds, and find it difficult, even impossible, to follow a daily work routine. Even if you appreciate order, somehow you just can't get yourself organized.

Overabundance of 4 Energy

You are overly rigid in your thinking, and can be bossy, stubborn, and dogmatic. You are too much of a disciplinarian, behaving at times like a battlefield general rather than an understanding superior. You easily become submerged in details, losing track of the big picture. You give the impression of being stodgy, stern, controlling, dull, and stuck in a rut. You may be motivated by deep-seated fear.

How I Rate Myself:

Lack   Balanced   Excess

My Experience of the Number 5

Balanced Expression of 5 Energy

Healthy 5 energy manifests as a progressive attitude and outlook. You are often ahead of the times in your field of expertise, and are usually adventurous, creative, multitalented, and versatile. You are an excellent communicator and salesperson, and have original ways of presenting your ideas. You enjoy working with people, have an entertaining and often fascinating personality, and are clever, witty, and analytical. You enjoy change and exploring new possibilities. Freedom is a key ingredient of your happiness.

Deficient or Underexpressed 5 Energy

You dislike change and are closed to new ideas, easily threatened by anything that might upset the status quo. You don't adapt well to new circumstances. You lack vision and imagination and don't function well outside of your routine. You fear life, adventure, risk, and new experiences.

Overabundance of 5 Energy

You are restless, inconsistent, and impatient, lacking in sustained effort, tending to quit situations and relationships before they reach completion. It is difficult for you to maintain a routine, and you may lack the discipline and perseverance required to reach your goals. Any new thing that comes along can throw you off course and cause you to lose focus. You overindulge in sensual pleasures, such as food, alcohol, drugs, or sex. You fail to learn from experience because you move on too quickly.

How I Rate Myself:

Lack   Balanced   Excess

My Experience of the Number 6

Balanced Expression of 6 Energy

You have a caring, friendly, sympathetic disposition, and enjoy helping others. You are conscientious and responsible, the one others turn to for help. Always ready to contribute to the betterment of the community, it is not uncommon to find you involved in some type of volunteer capacity. You have a strong sense of justice, artistic sensitivity, and may express healing ability. You are the ideal employee and an understanding manager, and you find fulfillment in a position of service. In all things, you seek stability, balance, and harmony.

Deficient or Underexpressed 6 Energy

Due to your difficulty in forming harmonious relationships with others, you struggle with solitude and unsatisfying relationships. Preferring to do things on your own, you try to avoid responsibilities and are fearful of making commitments to others. "Till death do us part" frightens you. It is difficult for you to express your true feelings, and so you remain guarded, preventing the development of trust required to sustain long-term relationships.

Overabundance of 6 Energy

You tend to be overly concerned with the welfare of others, fussing and worrying, even meddling and interfering in the affairs of others, extending yourself well beyond your personal boundaries. You can grow resentful of your responsibilities and obligations. You are jealous, possessive, suspicious, and demanding in love. You are overly idealistic, seeking perfection in yourself and in others. It is difficult for you to find balance.

How I Rate Myself:

Lack   Balanced   Excess

My Experience of the Number 7

Balanced Expression of 7 Energy

You have a strong mind, and tend to be deep, penetrating, analytical, and profound. You may also be very intuitive, although this attribute may not always be developed. You are inquisitive and intrigued by mystery, and you are a lover of knowledge. You may have an interest in spirituality, philosophy, and religion. You seem to be in some ways different from others, often marching to the beat of your own drum. You appreciate quiet and your time alone.

Deficient or Underexpressed 7 Energy

You prefer to remain on the surface of things, uninterested in digging for the deeper meaning of life. This prevents you from developing your full potential in many areas. You are not interested in the true meaning of situations. Ill-informed, you make inaccurate judgments and conclusions. You can be a slow learner.

Overabundance of 7 Energy

Overly involved with your own ideas and inner life, you show a lack of emotion, even coldness and superiority toward others. You can be overly analytical, suspicious, and tend to be highly critical and even intolerant of others. Others might think that you are a snob, since you prefer to be alone. Alienating others, you grow bitter and resentful of their lack of understanding of you.

How I Rate Myself:

Lack   Balanced   Excess

My Experience of the Number 8

Balanced Expression of 8 Energy

You are a strong and powerful force in your environment, commanding respect, allegiance, and obedience. Energetic, self-confident, and a good judge of character, you are well suited for the corporate world. You have clear ambitions and the drive, motivation, and organizational ability to reach your goals. You are practical, realistic, and dependable and can handle complex projects or situations.

Deficient or Underexpressed 8 Energy

You lack good judgment when it comes to money and possessions, causing you to experience fluctuations and material instability throughout your life. You fear your own power, and have difficulty with authority figures. Stubborn and impractical, you are resentful of being told what to do, yet powerless to reach your goals. You tend to be unrealistic, undisciplined, and lack ambition and drive.

Overabundance of 8 Energy

You are overly rigid, stubborn, selfish, combative, despotic, and materialistic. Your excessive ambition makes you insensitive to and impatient with others. Money, status, and power are very important to you, and you will seek these at any cost. You have a sense of entitlement, and can abuse the power invested in you, no matter how little it is.

How I Rate Myself:

My Experience of the Number 9

Balanced Expression of 9 Energy

You have universal appeal, and are someone that everyone likes. You are broad-minded, kind, fair, affectionate, and agreeable. You are imaginative and creative, and can be a bit overly idealistic. You can be a perfectionist, with yourself and with others. You enjoy participating in group or community projects, especially in anything that contributes to the well-being of the community at large. You don't mind setting your own interests aside for the welfare of others.

Deficient or Underexpressed 9 Energy

You lack sensitivity, compassion, and understanding, and don't deal well with emotions, either your own or other people's. You can be indifferent, uncooperative, and uncaring. You tend to be self-centered, unkind, unforgiving, and intolerant. It is difficult for you to set your own ambitions and needs aside for those of others. You have a narrow, rigid outlook on life and don't adapt well to new ideas.

Overabundance of 9 Energy

You tend to be a daydreamer and can be naïve, impractical, unrealistic, and overly emotional—a "diva" of sorts, demanding to have your every little whim catered to. You can be inconsistent, petty, changeful, and uncooperative. You may blame others and the world for your situation, while it is your own unwillingness to assume responsibility for yourself that is the cause of your problems.

How I Rate Myself:

Lack   Balanced   Excess

TWO

✦ ✦ ✦

Your Birth Date

A PERSONAL LIFE ROAD MAP

The Life Path Number

Among the numbers derived from your Birth Date, the
Life Path number is by far the most important as it describes the terrain of your life's journey. Knowledge of
this number, how it manifests in your life, and how you
make use of its qualities and attributes is an essential
component to determining your success. Some roads
are hilly, others have sharp curves and bends, and others are relatively flat. Some trace the rugged coastline,
others climb high into the mountains, while others cut
through golden prairies.

> *A good plan is like a road
> map: it shows the final
> destination and usually
> the best way to get there.*
>
> H. STANLEY JUDD

Depending on the nature of the road you must travel, you will modify your approach
to your journey. Each person's path is unique and should be approached in accordance
with needs, age, and experience. What is easy for one may be challenging for another.
Then again, what may have been challenging at one point in your life may have become
easy with age, maturity, and experience. Hence the benefits of periodically standing back
and doing an exercise such as "Where Am I Now?" at the end of this chapter.

Your Life Path number essentially describes the nature of the opportunities as well as
the lessons and challenges you are likely to encounter along the way. Difficult stretches

of road may require careful attention, but at the same time can motivate you to be more resourceful and creative, pushing you to make greater use of your talents and abilities. Smooth, straight roads are easy to navigate, but can also become boring and lacking in personal rewards as they are less challenging, requiring less use of talents and abilities. In working with clients, I have observed that overly easy periods can bring about less progress and fewer accomplishments than challenging ones, which require that you dig deep and work much harder. On the other hand, when used productively, smooth, easy stretches can be very helpful in giving you the opportunity to rest, stand back, and re-group. Taking a breather now and then can be very worthwhile.

Understanding the nature of your Life Path, with its periodic twists and turns, will enable you to not only have a clearer picture of your destination, but also plot a more effective course toward your intended goals.

Calculating the Life Path Number

The Life Path number is easy to calculate. First reduce the numbers of your Month, Day, and Year of birth to single digits. Then add these numbers, and again reduce to a single digit. As mentioned in chapter 1, the numbers 11 and 22 are not reduced. For example, for a person whose Birth Date is June 29, 1971, you would proceed as follows:

1. Month of birth: June, 6th month.

2. Day of birth: 29 = 2 + 9 = 11 (Master number, do not reduce).

3. Year of birth: 1971 = 1 + 9 + 7 + 1= 18, reduce, 1 + 8 = 9.

4. Add the reduced numbers from the Month, Day, and Year of birth, 6 + 11 + 9 = 26, reduce to a single digit, 2 + 6 = 8. The Life Path for this person is 8.

How to Calculate the Life Path Number

Example for a person born June 29, 1971.

	A	B	C
Birth Month	6	6	6
Birth Day	29	2+9	11
Birth Year	1971	1+9+7+1	9
Sum of numbers in column C			26
Reduce sum to single digit		2 + 6 = 8	

The Life Path is 8.

Note if there is a Karmic Debt number behind the Life Path, a 14 *behind* a 5, for example. This will have a bearing on how the energies of the Life Path are likely to be manifested. A certain amount of conscious effort may be required before the full positive range and potential of your Life Path can be expressed.

An example calculation for a person born August 12, 1956:

1. Month of birth: August, 8th month.

2. Day of birth: 12 = 1 + 2 = 3.

3. Year of birth: 1956 = 1 + 9 + 5 + 6 = 21, reduce, 2 + 1 = 3.

4. Add the reduced numbers from the Month, Day, and Year of birth, 8 + 3 + 3 = 14, reduce to a single digit, 1 + 4 = 5. Note the presence of a Karmic Debt number. The Life Path for this person is 14/5.

Exercise: Calculate Your Life Path Number

Calculate Your Life Path Number

	A	B	C
Birth Month	_____	_____	_____
Birth Day	_____	_____	_____
Birth Year	_____	_____	_____
Sum of numbers in column C			_____
Reduce sum to single digit	_____		

The 1 Life Path

This is the Life Path of the individualist. You are driven by pure energy, which is often manifested in leadership skills and entrepreneurial spirit, as well as a great need for independence. You are self-motivated, autonomous, pioneering, resourceful, imaginative, inventive, creative, and goal oriented. Before you can fully manifest your potential, you may need to develop confidence in your abilities and tap into the natural self-reliance that is part of your nature. Experience and maturity will bring you what you need to be successful.

Individuals with the 1 Life Path are ready and prepared to focus on their goals and ambitions. You prefer to make your own way in life with as little support from others as possible. Your independent nature can prove to be a blessing, as it enables you to forge ahead, but at times it can be a curse, as you can disregard the needs of others while seeking to reach your own goals. Your journey often involves the breaking of new ground in your field of expertise. You do not easily seek out the help of mentors, preferring to make it on your own. You may be concerned with how you appear to others, wanting to give a good impression, one that smacks of success. Your pride can hold you back; you need to be reminded that sometimes it's okay to ask for help.

You can at times forget to look beyond your own boundaries and may even become uncaring or selfish. The conscious development of an awareness of the world outside yourself can be very beneficial. Your interests are varied, and your potential for success is enormous. Occupational fields include business, management, the arts, and community affairs, all areas in which you can be creative and express a leadership role.

If you have a Karmic Debt 19 behind your 1 Life Path, you may struggle with large-scale dreams and a desire to satisfy your own personal desires. You need to find a balance between tending to your needs and being sensitive and aware of the needs of others. You should guard against a tendency to be overly aggressive, trampling over others to reach your goals. There may be times when you feel alone and unsupported, but then again, you are often too proud and stubborn to ask for help. There is tremendous potential for creative leadership and personal success with this Life Path number, once its lessons have been learned.

If you have a 1 Life Path child, consider encouraging his or her self-reliance and independence. A healthy sense of self-awareness should be cultivated rather than inhibited, otherwise feelings of resentment and frustration could emerge in misguided outbursts or even an outright battle against authority. At the same time, 1 Life Path children are naturally inclined to focus on themselves and need to be taught to be considerate and compassionate toward others.

The 2 Life Path

You are very sensitive to the needs of others, conciliatory in style, and an excellent companion, listener, mediator, and moderator. You long to be in the ideal relationship and prefer to do things in the company of others. You may not do as well in a solo enterprise as would a 1 or 5 Life Path unless it is a service-based business, in which case you are likely to excel. Sometimes you tend to set your own needs aside in favor of the needs of others. This can lead you to make questionable choices of partnerships and relationships. You can be somewhat shy and sensitive and generally do not seek the limelight for yourself, preferring the anonymity of a behind-the-scenes role. You are highly perceptive, patient, diplomatic, and cooperative and can be quite content helping your partner attain success.

You have a genuine concern for the welfare of others, and are often the first to step up to help a friend in need. You are dependable, responsible, reliable, caring, thoughtful, loyal, and devoted. You are also adaptable and flexible. You prefer the comfort of quiet, peaceful environments. Individuals with the 2 Life Path make excellent therapists, peacemakers, teachers, counselors, trainers, support staff members, aids, coaches, partners, mentors, mediators, and healers. They make great administrative assistants.

Children with the 2 Life Path are very sensitive to the comments and even the mere facial or bodily expressions of their caregivers. They can take things far too personally, and they need to be taught early in life that everything isn't always about them. They can be shy and will keep things inside for fear of what others might say or think. They are affectionate and eager to please others and will thrive in a peaceful, loving, and harmonious environment. They prefer the company of others to solitude.

The 3 Life Path

You have excellent communication skills, a lively and positive outlook, resilience, lots of charm, wit, and enormous creative potential. Individuals with the 3 Life Path are artists by nature and often excel in some form of creative self-expression. Sometimes these talents remain dormant, or are consciously set aside for many years and can, in a later, more quiet time of life, flourish into a very enriching and rewarding hobby or even second career. Success in the arts requires discipline and dedication, attributes that don't come naturally to many 3s, and will have to be developed. You are a born entertainer, and are very often the life of the party.

You have more than your share of grace, style, and social skills. You are optimistic, a great motivator, easy-going, and like to enjoy life. You are naturally emotional and volatile, and can express your thoughts freely. Be aware of a tendency to be gossipy and superficial. You prefer to talk about a subject superficially rather than research it thoroughly. Managing your own finances can be a challenge. You can be vulnerable, dramatic, and sensitive to criticism, and at times you can be your own worst critic. You can be easily distracted and may lose track of your long-term goals. A hands-on, short-term approach may be helpful if you are having difficulty sticking to your plans. You can do well in sales, and all the arts, media, communications, and entertainment fields.

Children with the 3 Life Path are sociable and enjoy the company of others. They enjoy fun and play, and can find it difficult to focus on homework and other limiting activities. They are affectionate and tend to express themselves freely. However, they can say things off the top of their heads, sometimes not mindful of how their words might affect others, and they should be taught to think before speaking. They need to learn to not hog the stage. They also should be taught to be responsible and organized.

The 4 Life Path

You are no doubt very well organized, hard working, grounded, and you may welcome, even expect, structure and order in all things. Areas of life that are important to you include family, home, financial and material security, and stability. This is usually not the path of the risk taker. You do well in a structured environment, with a regular schedule, and can thrive in the routine of a nine-to-five workday. You must guard against becoming overly rigid and close-minded in your habits, opinions, and attitudes.

You may be fearful of change and hesitant to venture out into the world, limiting your experiences to known environments, even becoming a homebody. You don't mind working at home, even out of your basement. You flourish in jobs that require attention to detail and service. Individuals with the 4 Life Path can be found in banking, finance, business, building, and all activities requiring organization and order. They are loyal, dedicated, trustworthy, reliable, honest, and not afraid of hard work. They are the workhorses of any enterprise or organization.

When there is a 13/4 Karmic Debt behind your Life Path, your life journey may seem unusually fraught with obstacles, challenges, and limitations. You often lack self-confidence and can be profoundly fearful. You struggle under the heavy mantle of hard work. If you would simply buckle down and focus on the tasks at hand, you would find great rewards in your eventual accomplishments. You can be overly rigid in your attitudes and habits. Opinionated and close-minded, you may miss opportunities by clutching to old patterns and behaviors. By developing self-confidence and a positive and open-minded attitude, you can be among the hardest working and most productive of all.

Children with the 4 Life Path are focused and hard working by nature. They need a secure and orderly home to feel safe, and they respond well to stability and routine. They can be taught the value of dedication, practice, and regularity. They do well in a structured and disciplined environment. But all work and no play can make junior a bit stiff, so he must also be taught that it's okay to schedule time for fun and play.

The 5 Life Path

You enjoy change, variety, and movement. You usually don't do well in office jobs. The nine-to-five cubicle is not the place for you! Although day-to-day routine is not your forte, you can work twice as long and twice as hard as anybody in an activity for which you feel a passion. You need to move about, always seeking excitement, new challenges, and stimulus. You must guard against changing for the sake of change alone. Prone to risk taking, you tend to jump into new ventures without adequate forethought.

Freedom is key to this Life Path. You may feel resentful and become uncooperative if you find yourself trapped in an overly restrictive environment. You need to learn that in order to achieve anything of significance, you must develop constancy, dedication, and diligence. You are multitalented and can do many things well. You gravitate toward adventure, innovation, careers involving communications, teaching, and entertainment, and given your need for freedom, you can do well as a self-employed worker and sales rep, provided you acquire enough discipline and order to work efficiently. You are flexible, original, very resourceful, adaptable, and creative. You like to live well and large, enjoying all the pleasures that life has to offer. Beware of a tendency to overindulge in food, drink, and physical pleasures. You can be disorganized and lacking in focus.

If there is a Karmic Debt 14 behind your 5 Life Path, this can indicate a more erratic and irregular journey. You lack forethought and can make impulsive decisions, which lead to error. You have difficulty completing what you start, being easily led to newer, more exciting opportunities, and can fail to learn from experience. You fear limitation and avoid making long-term commitments, preferring personal freedom to devotion and dedication to service or job. You need to learn the benefits of sustained and committed efforts; otherwise, you will repeatedly fall short of your goals. Once your lessons are learned, you can successfully express your tremendous versatility, broad range of talents and abilities, innovation, and creativity in your career.

Children with the 5 Life Path need to be given opportunities to experiment and explore a variety of avenues throughout childhood. They are inquisitive, adventurous, and innovative. Strong individualists, they prefer to do things at their own pace and in their own way, and should not be held to the same standards of measure as their siblings or peers. Although quick learners, they may at times lose focus due to a tendency to seek freedom or excitement outside the daily routine of home and school. They have a very low threshold for boredom, and don't do well in overly rigid environments. They need to be taught the benefits of order and structure.

The 6 Life Path

Loving, caring, and kind, you naturally enjoy responsibility. You are socially involved, eager to be of help, and genuinely concerned with the welfare of others. The 6s are the nurturers, supporters, and caregivers of the world. You feel validated when in a position of service and helpfulness to others, and in fact need to be needed. You can easily become indispensable in your job or home environment. However, in your desire to be helpful, you can overextend your boundaries and interfere in the affairs of others, becoming more meddlesome than helpful. Many 6s should learn discernment in their eagerness to help and to please others, otherwise they can become resentful of their extensive responsibilities. Know that it is not necessary to save the world in order to be loved.

You have excellent executive abilities as well as a fair dose of artistic sensitivity and creativity. You are charming, gentle, affectionate, and friendly. Individuals with the 6 Life Path make excellent managers. You are an able problem solver—fair, just, and reliable. Areas of interest include management, sales, service-based industries, the health fields and the healing arts, social work, teaching, the arts, human resources, consulting, customer service, entertainment, and hospitality.

Children with the 6 Life Path are affectionate and want to please parents and teachers. They can be the teacher's pets, and everyone's friends. They make friends easily, and can at times compromise their own judgment for the sake of having a place among friends. Stronger personality types can influence them. They need to be taught to stick to their own values, even at the risk of losing a friend along the way. The 6 Life Path often has creative and artistic abilities.

The 7 Life Path

This is the Life Path of the analyst, the philosopher, and the thinker. You are generally quiet, low-key, somewhat secretive, and sometimes shy, at least in your younger years. You may choose to avoid drawing attention to yourself, preferring the safety of your spot in the corner, and can appear distant and aloof. Your challenge in life is to keep your personal life private while dealing with the affairs of the outside world. You can be quite comfortable working alone, preferring isolated, quiet environments. In fact, for the sake of your well-being, you need your alone time. Your tendency to withdraw into seclusion when you have personal issues can alienate others. You may be cold and rational in personal relationships, preferring not to express your feelings.

You must learn to be comfortable in your solitude, without feeling lonely. For that, a healthy dose of self-love and self-respect is required. You can become critical of others, even to the point of feeling superior. A positive attitude should be cultivated and maintained at all times. Often, feelings of specialness or of being different are experienced with this Life Path. You are a seeker of truth, knowledge, and understanding. You enjoy uncovering mysteries and thrive when intellectually challenged. You can do well as a researcher, writer, teacher, expert, consultant, scholar, healer, therapist, analyst, priest, counselor, problem solver, or investigator.

If you have a 16 Karmic Debt, you no doubt have additional lessons to learn. Subject to intense introspection and analysis, you may experience one or more important transformations in your life, akin to the phoenix rising from its ashes. Often, this lesson involves a reversal of financial fortune, or the experience of a Dark Night of the Soul. It is important that you look beyond the superficial and material and focus on integrating the deeper meaning of things. You may suffer intense shyness and self-consciousness. You must guard against a tendency toward cynicism, jealousy, mistrust, self-centeredness, excessive pride, and feelings of specialness and superiority. Trust and faith are among your most important lessons. By accepting responsibility and developing trust in others, by being kind-hearted and compassionate, you will experience a deeply rewarding life.

Children with the 7 Life Path enjoy their time alone, playing quietly with their toys, enjoying time away from the hustle and bustle of school and organized social events. They need intellectual challenges and puzzles to thrive. They have many questions, but may keep them to themselves, not wanting to draw undue attention. They must learn to open up in a safe environment, with someone who will not criticize or analyze them. Being overly analytical, a positive and supportive environment is especially important during the early years.

The 8 Life Path

You have plenty of natural leadership abilities, charm, energy, and drive. You have definite ambitions for personal success and wealth; you work well with a plan and have specific goals and objectives to meet. You are practical, hands-on, and down-to-earth. Eight is the number of power and worldly success. You will probably not be content until you have achieved something of importance. Individuals with the 8 Life Path tend to think big, talk big, act big, and like to look successful. Many 8s are actually the movers and the shakers of the world, the ones that make things happen.

You can be overbearing once you set out to reach your goals, sometimes trampling over anything and anyone that might stand in your way. You can be the proverbial bull in a china shop. You can be too busy with the big picture to see the small things in front of you. You must learn to consider the welfare of others as well as your own interests in all your undertakings. If you are an insecure 8, you can become frustrated at your inherent lack of power, taking power wherever you can find it, usually over those who are weaker than you. An 8 without a good working plan is likely to be frustrated and unhappy. They need to see results, the bottom line. A healthy 8 Life Path expresses itself as inspiration, leadership, motivation, and focused drive. It is the path of the entrepreneur, leader, manager, CEO, or director.

Children with the 8 Life Path want to go to the head of the class before they can walk! They do well if given tasks that will make them feel important and responsible. They don't do well standing at the back of the class waiting their turn while the others get their chance to show their talents. They need to learn empathy and compassion, two traits that will serve them well over time. They understand the concept of responsibility very early on and can thrive on having important tasks assigned to them.

The 9 Life Path

You are a humanitarian at heart, a visionary, and you are sensitive and socially conscious. You have a deep-seated desire to do something to make the world a better place. You are idealistic, creative, kind-hearted, artistic, and imaginative. If you don't have a function in the world or the community, you will look for ways of expressing your generous nature by helping those who are close at hand. In a world of overwhelming materialism, this is not always an easy Life Path to fulfill. You are open to lending an ear; you are a great problem solver and can express compassion and understanding. You have a genuine concern for the welfare of others and can see the big picture in all things. Your idealism can lead you to be disappointed with the mediocre ways of the world.

Individuals with the 9 Life Path generally enjoy travel, and many will travel far and wide for their work or for pleasure. You can become discouraged by the harshness of events in the world and can be profoundly disturbed by images of war, hunger, violence, cruelty, or sickness. At times, your broad outlook can make you feel superior to others. You need to understand that your happiness depends on your ability to be self-less and to think of the greater good. Selfishness in the 9 leads to profound frustration, resentment, and unhappiness. Selflessness leads to feelings of joy and fulfillment.

Children with the 9 Life Path are sensitive to the needs and expressions of the people around them. They have refined minds and can thrive in a broad, renaissance-style education. They are idealistic, easily connect with nature and the arts, and can be perfectionists at work and play. They need to learn to accept things as they are, imperfect as they are. They also need to understand that they cannot change the world in an instant.

The 11/2 Life Path

You have many of the attributes of the 2 Life Path, but are much more emotionally charged and sensitive, as though plugged into a higher energy source. This intense energy can manifest physically, creating tension and sensitivity to the environment, but it is mostly felt mentally and emotionally. You may be inspired by inner guidance, or a higher source, and can in turn inspire others. Highly emotional and intuitive, you may find it difficult to be moderate or to adopt a middle ground in anything that you do. You are very idealistic, and sometimes impractical or unrealistic in the goals you set for yourself. You may perceive yourself as having a special purpose in life, sensing that you are different from others, with a unique mission to accomplish. You must guard against developing an overly inflated sense of self-importance and specialness.

Individuals with the 11 Life Path often have difficulty staying connected to reality. You need to develop sufficient confidence and inner strength to feel comfortable with your life purpose. You will do better with a few years' experience under your belt. When expressed in a balanced manner, 11s can be profoundly inspired to contribute in an important way to the betterment of a unique aspect of the human experience. (Read also the description of the 2 Life Path.)

The 22/4 Life Path

You are the Master Builder, and since a young age you may have sensed a burning desire to accomplish something of great value and importance. You want to change the world and in some way make a difference. Your opportunities may appear limited in comparison to your desire for accomplishment. You have great management, organizational, and executive ability and the skill set required to bring large projects to completion. The potential of this Life Path is not easily expressed, especially in youth. It usually takes many years of hard work and dedication to come to full expression. Few people actualize the full potential of this number early in life and many never achieve it at all. Individuals with the 22 Life Path are most successful when they go outside the common ways of doing things, using their creativity and imagination to find unique ways of achieving their goals. (Read also the description of the 4 Life Path.)

The Birth Day Number

The number of the day on which you were born, included in the calculation of your Life Path number, provides additional information about your nature. It describes particular attributes or talents that you can call on. For example, if you were born on the third of any month, your Birth Day number would be 3; on the twenty-ninth of any month, it would be 2 + 9, or 11 (11/2); on the nineteenth, 1 + 9 = 10, 1 + 0, or 1. Although of lesser importance than the Life Path number, it can provide clues as to which type of career or job would best allow you to manifest your talents. Note in particular if your Birth Day is a Master number, 11 or 22, or a Karmic Debt number, 13, 14, 16, or 19.

1, 10, 19, and 28 Birth Days

If you have a 1 Birth Day, you strive to be independent and autonomous. You are ambitious, willful, dynamic, energetic, and forward thinking. At the same time, you are practical and creative, an excellent combination for leadership positions. You have excellent potential for achieving your goals. You are often an inspiration to others. However, 1s, and in particular the 19, need to guard against excessive willfulness and selfishness that can lead to insensitivity to others.

2, 11, 20, and 29 Birth Days

If you have a 2 Birth Day, you are an excellent mediator and a peacemaker, sensitive to the needs of others. You are the ideal partner and team player. You do well as a healer, teacher, and support staff member; the power behind the throne. In general, 2s are affectionate and caring, but they can be moody and insecure. Also, 11s and 29s (which reduce to 11) exhibit additional sensitivity to the environment as well as a sense of specialness. They will often seek to distinguish themselves in some unique way.

3, 12, 21, and 30 Birth Days

You are generally friendly, loving, caring, enthusiastic, affectionate, and sociable. You are probably creative and imaginative, though you enjoy a practical and hands-on job. You are an excellent communicator and an original thinker, optimistic and energetic. Individuals with 3 Birth Days often do well in the arts and entertainment fields. You can be scattered, gossipy, and superficial. You may hide your true feelings.

4, 13, 22, and 31 Birth Days

Individuals with 4 Birth Days are excellent organizers and hard workers—they are conscientious, dedicated, steadfast, structured, rational, and practical. If you have a 4 Birth Day, you can be rigid in your habits and in your thinking, sometimes lacking originality and spontaneity. You are comfortable with routine and order and have a knack for detailed work. The 13 in particular needs to guard against excessive negativity, stubbornness, and rigidity. If your birthday is on the twenty-second of the month, you have the additional influence of a Master number, which gives you a desire to make a difference in the world. This is the number of the Master Builder—22s can handle very large undertakings.

5, 14, and 23 Birth Days

If your Birth Day is a 5, you need adventure, variety, change, and lots of freedom. You are versatile and a quick learner, original and progressive in your thinking. You generally do not like routine and restriction. You can be impatient and inconsistent. You are an excellent teacher or communicator. If your birthday is on the fourteenth of the month, you will need to learn order, discipline, and dedication, otherwise you will find it difficult to reach your goals.

6, 15, and 24 Birth Days

If you have a 6 Birth Day, you thrive in positions of responsibility. You are a people person, always helpful and attentive to the concerns of others, and are an excellent manager. You are friendly, affectionate, loving, practical, and genuinely caring. You are emotional, and can at times become overly involved in the affairs of others, sometimes meddling. At times, you can be resentful of your responsibilities.

7, 16, and 25 Birth Days

If you have a 7 Birth Day, you enjoy your solitude. You are a deep, analytical thinker and an excellent problem solver. You like mysteries and need to be intellectually challenged. The 16 adds an element of specialness, feelings of being different. Sometimes you can feel superior. In general, 7s can be uncomfortable in emotional situations, and 16s in particular can shy away from intimacy for fear of revealing their true feelings.

8, 17, and 26 Birth Days

If your birthday falls on an 8 day, you have a mind for business and the corporate world may be for you. You have organizational, managerial, administrative, and leadership abilities. Ambitious, energetic, dependable, reliable, focused, and driven, you thrive in a position of power and authority. You have an eye for the big picture and should delegate the detailed work. In your desire to reach your goals, you can be insensitive to others, even uncaring.

9, 18, and 27 Birth Days

If you have a 9 Birth Day, you are generous and kind-hearted, broad-minded, and sensitive to the needs of others—a humanitarian. You are creative and imaginative, and may have artistic abilities. You have great potential for success in the world. You can be emotional and dramatic, sometimes not knowing what to do with your deep feelings. At times, you can be overly generous, and may become resentful when your giving is not returned in kind.

Your Future Starts Now

Before we get into the business of mapping out future trends, you may want to pause and reflect on your current situation. A prerequisite to making effective decisions for the future is that you first acknowledge where you have come from, recognize how you arrived at your present circumstances, and then take stock of where you are in your life at the moment. Past decisions and actions determined where you are now, and your present and upcoming decisions will determine your future. The more you know and accept yourself, the more likely you will be to make decisions that will reflect your true desires and ultimately take your life in the direction of personal fulfillment.

With your Life Path and Birth Day numbers, you are probably beginning to have a much clearer picture of your journey. For example, if you have a number 4 Life Path, you may have a tendency to make decisions based on material insecurity and fear of scarcity. No matter how bright your trends for the future, you are likely to take a moderate approach to rising opportunities. If, on the other hand, you are strongly marked by the number 5's need for freedom and change, you may experience frustration and limitation during a period of 4 influence.

> *Destiny is not a matter of chance, it is a matter of choice; it is not a thing to be waited for, it is a thing to be achieved.*
>
> WILLIAM JENNINGS BRYAN

Being aware of past behaviors, you can modify your approach, leading to better opportunities and results. This way, you are better equipped to take on the challenges and opportunities presented by an upcoming trend, thus actively participating in the creation of a better future for yourself. In the previous example, addressing your material insecurity and fear of scarcity issues by taking appropriate measures such as sitting down with an advisor and laying out a financial plan, perhaps combined with positive affirmations, may prepare you to rise to greater, bolder challenges in the future. You could then take advantage of excellent opportunities for growth, which you might otherwise have avoided.

Perhaps you have a job, maybe even a good job by today's market standards, but you feel somehow limited, unhappy with your present occupation and clueless as to where to go next. You have a sense of having missed opportunities, or that something is lacking in your life. You don't know where to turn, or how long your present situation of loss and confusion will last.

Entrepreneurs approach obstacles and challenges differently from the average working person. The charts of entrepreneurs I have found tend to be more challenged than the charts of people who are comfortably employed, offering on the one hand, more possibilities for growth, while on the other hand, more chances of staying blocked. Even if they find themselves in the wrong business, as happens many times with a first attempt at entrepreneurship, there is usually a positive outcome from the experience, such as an important lesson learned about their abilities, limits, and capabilities.

Many boomers are quitting their jobs of twenty-plus years and venturing into the world of entrepreneurship. Many of these people know themselves well, they know what they like, they know what they want, and they know what they are good at. They also know what they don't like and don't want, but not always what they are not good at. They generally think they can do it all. Although the prospect of jumping into an uncertain world can appear frightening, they stand on the confidence of past experience and acquired knowledge, a powerful force that fuels them onward. It takes a fair amount of courage to make the leap from the security of a job to the uncertain world of the self-employed.

Today's job market is fiercely competitive. It is all the more important that the individual ensures that he is employing his best assets in his job. People perform best when they are doing what they are good at. The employee, in comparison to the self-employed worker, has a different set of challenges to address when considering matters such as life purpose, direction, and personal growth and satisfaction. He must manage his life and goals within the context of the company or organization for which he works. His efforts are often underappreciated or even not recognized by his superiors, who are themselves overwhelmed by responsibilities and stresses of their own.

The employee must derive satisfaction by setting personal goals and recognizing his own worth within those of the group culture. There are times when the employee realizes that his goals are no longer in alignment with the values of the company. He may force himself to fit into this now-foreign environment, sometimes for years, setting into motion a pattern of negative growth and dissatisfaction. Many employees leave their jobs because the stress of working in an unsuitable environment has taken its toll. This can manifest as a burnout or other health-related issue, or marital breakdown, and often both. Seldom is poor performance on the job the initial cause.

Exercise: Where Am I Now?

My Life Path number	
My Birth Day number	

Now, with the knowledge of your Life Path and Birth Day numbers, you are beginning to lay down the foundation for mapping out your life journey. This knowledge will help you make choices that are more appropriate, given your particular talents, abilities, and inclinations. You may belong to the significant number of people who are not

> *Success is liking yourself, liking what you do, and liking how you do it.*
> MAYA ANGELOU

living the life of their dreams, who experience a feeling of something missing in their lives, or who have some level of unmet hopes and expectations. No matter your situation, keeping your numbers in mind, ask yourself a few questions to shed light on where you are before we look at upcoming trends and start to plan where you are going next.

- Is my job/career satisfactory? If not, why not?

- How do I define success for myself?

- Have I attained the goals I set out for myself many years ago?

- Am I tending to all the important areas of my life? If not, which are being ignored, and why? Which are outdated? Why am I holding on to outdated activities?

- What are my long-term goals for myself? My family? My business? My retirement?

- On a scale of one to ten, how would I rate my life overall at this time?

- If I could wave a magic wand, what would I change in my life?

- Do my lifestyle and career reflect the potential of my Life Path and Birth Day numbers? If not, what could I do to be more in tune with the energies of my numbers?

THREE

Mapping the Journey

GOAL SETTING AND THE 9-YEAR EPICYCLE

Effective planning and goal setting has become one of the key ingredients in all success formulas. Making lists of short- and long-term goals and creating picture books are among some of the popular tools for those wanting to have a more hands-on approach to attracting success and abundance into their lives. Being aware of your numerology cycles *in addition* to goal setting, planning, coaching, positive habits, etc., will greatly enhance your chances of success. As stated in the last chapter, your Life Path number provides the foundation for your journey, establishing the general tone of the opportunities and experiences you are likely to encounter along the way. Having been introduced to your Life Path, you can now begin to map out the details of your journey.

In this chapter, we will focus on the second set of numbers derived from your date of birth, the numbers concerned with the short- to mid-term trends found in the 9-Year Epicycle. These are the most exciting and powerful numbers to work with in planning and goal setting as they describe events, circumstances, situations, lessons, and challenges encountered on a yearly, monthly, and daily basis. The 9-Year Epicycle maps out, if you will, the details of your journey. These numbers include:

- The Personal Year

- The Personal Month

- The Personal Day

The 9-Year Epicycle, also known as the Personal Year Cycle, is a powerful tool not only for establishing an effective long-term plan, but also for gauging your growth and accomplishment levels over time. This cycle is broken down into individual years, from 1 to 9, each with its own climate and tendencies, called Personal Years. The years are then considered on a month-by-month basis, again each with its own numerical value from 1 to 9, giving us the Personal Month numbers. Finally, for added information, you can include Personal Day numbers for daily trends.

The cycle begins with a 1 Personal Year, a time of renewed energy and new beginnings. From the 1 Year, the cycle progresses and develops through each year until it reaches its peak at the 8 Personal Year, at which point the rewards of the efforts of the past seven years are reaped. The cycle winds down with the 9 Year, a period of rest, ideally a sabbatical, during which, time should be spent finishing off projects, integrating learning and slowing down activity, thus clearing the way for the next epicycle beginning the following year.

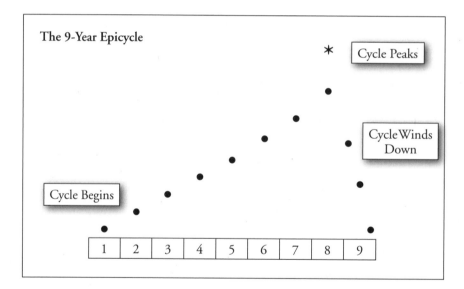

If you are in the first three years of an epicycle, you are in the early planning and development stage, and can focus on establishing a new direction on which you will build long-term goals. This is the time to explore, experiment, consider your options, and expand into new horizons. In other words, you have the benefit of time on your side.

In the middle stage, the fourth to sixth years, plans and projects should be well underway and solidly established. You are now in the thick of it, and should focus on doing whatever it takes so that you can attain tangible results. Make any necessary adjustments, establish a practical system or method, and focus on the work at hand.

During the final three years of the cycle, you should concentrate on bringing your projects to a close. This is not the time to quit; you are close to the finish line now. You may be inclined to look ahead toward where you want to go next and begin to consider your next set of long-term goals. Take the time to finish things off first. You are running out of time as your current cycle winds down to a close. If you have been working with specific goals in mind and hope to experience success, now is the time to hunker down and give it all you've got. Although time is running out, you have the benefit of experience on your side now.

The 3 Stages of the 9-Year Epicycle

Initiate, Renew, Develop			Build, Grow, Consolidate			Achieve, Integrate, Conclude		
1	2	3	4	5	6	7	8	9

If you are reaching the end of your epicycle and realize that you are far from achieving the goals you set for yourself years earlier, you may want to consider making adjustments. Trim back the fat. Aim for more realistic goals, so that in the end you will experience a certain degree of satisfaction. If you have aimed too high, you could end up feeling frustrated or discouraged should you fail to achieve your goals, reinforcing negative attitudes about your ability to be successful. Coming from a place of failure, it will make it all the more difficult for you to set new goals once your next cycle begins. It's better for your confidence and self-esteem to successfully achieve a lesser goal than to aim for and fail at a larger one. By consistently setting realistic goals that reflect where you are on your journey, you will experience your life as a series of successes rather than failed attempts. Don't be like those who spend a long life in waiting for success to miraculously happen.

The 9-Year Epicycle has a beginning phase motivated by a sense of optimism, new possibilities, and opportunities; a productive middle phase filled with work, expansion, and responsibility; and a final third phase of accomplishment, rewards, and completion.

By keeping the natural progression of the 9-Year Epicycle in mind when establishing goals, your projects will flow more smoothly and you will feel less challenged by obstacles and delays. You will feel more in control and more confident, things will work better, and you will view most situations from a realistic perspective.

The Personal Year Number

The Personal Year number can be used as a sort of signpost along the road, indicating road conditions, curves, bumps, and points of interest for the part of your journey that lasts for the duration of one calendar year. The manner in which one person experiences a certain set of circumstances may be different from another's experience of the same. It is therefore important to base your interpretations and decisions on your personal life journey as well as on your present level of learning and life experience rather than on a generalized formula. When interpreting meanings for your trends, remember to apply them to your personal context. Your life will not suddenly change course and turn into someone else's journey just because your trends have changed. If, for example, you have determined that the number 2 is a prominent influence in your life, but the energy of the number 1 is lacking, it does not mean that because you are in a 1 Personal Year all of a sudden you will become daring, adventurous, and independent. You could in fact feel a bit nervous in a 1 Personal Year, facing the uncertainty of new opportunities.

Also keep in mind that not all days, months, and years contain events of major importance in our lives. Sometimes, several forgettable years can pass by before anything of importance occurs. Also, numbers do not define with absolute certainty the nature and outcome of every event, nor do they predict with fated certainty the result of all your decisions. The various cycles described by your numbers indicate likely tendencies, lessons to be learned, and potential trends. Whether or not you are comfortable with the energy of a particular number will determine how you will deal with it when it becomes active in your life. (See the exercise in chapter 1: "My Experience of the Numbers.")

Calculating the Personal Year Number

To calculate the Personal Year number for a given year, first reduce the numbers of the Birth Day, Month, and Year to a single digit. Note that if the result is either 11 or 22, do not reduce to a single digit. For example, for a person with a birthday on June 29, you would calculate the Personal Year number for 2006 as follows:

1. Birth Month: June, 6th month.

2. Birth Day: 29 = 2 + 9 = 11, do not reduce.

3. Calendar Year: 2006, 2 + 0 + 0 + 6 = 8.

4. Add the results for the Month, Day, and Year: 6 + 11 + 8 = 25.

5. Reduce the total to a single digit or Master number: 2 + 5 = 7. The Personal Year number for 2006 for someone whose birthday is June 29 is 7.

How to Calculate the Personal Year
Example for 2006 for a person whose birthday is June 29.

	A	**B**	**C**
Birth Month	6	6	6
Birth Day	29	2+9	11
Current Year	2006	2+6	8
Sum of numbers in column C			25
Reduce sum to single digit		2 + 5 = 7	

The Personal Year number is 7.

Note that Karmic Debts are not considered when calculating the Personal Year numbers. The Personal Year begins in January and ends in December. For detailed descriptions as well as yearly planning exercises for each Personal Year, see chapters 4–12.

Exercise: Calculate Your Personal Year Number

The Personal Year

	A	B	C
Birth Month	____	____	____
Birth Day	____	____	____
Current Year	____	____	____
Sum of numbers in column C			____
Reduce sum to single digit		_____	

The Personal Month Number

The Personal Month number provides helpful information for planning your year on a month-by-month basis. It will not change or significantly modify the trends indicated by your Personal Year number, but it will help focus its energy into productive areas of activity. To calculate a Personal Month, add the Calendar Month, reduced to a single digit or Master number, and the Personal Year number. For example, the Personal Month for December, for a person whose Personal Year is 7:

1. Personal Year: 7.

2. Calendar Month: December, 12th month = 1 + 2 = 3.

3. Add the Personal Year number to the Calendar Month number: 7 + 3 = 10 = 1.

How to Calculate the Personal Month

Example for December for a person whose Personal Year is 7.

	A	B	C
Current Personal Year	7	7	7
Calendar Month	12	1+2	3
Sum of numbers in column C			10
Reduce sum to single digit		1	

The Personal Month number is 1.

For the interpretation of your Personal Months, consider Master numbers as well as Karmic Debts. The energy of the Personal Month begins on the first of the month and ends on the last day. Its influence peaks in the two middle weeks of the month and wanes in the last few days.

You will note from the following table that the 6, 7, 8, and 9 Personal Years each contain a complete nine-month cycle. These years are important in that they are a time when much accomplishment is possible. When you have reached the 6 Personal Year, initial research, study, and preliminary work should have been completed, and you may want to focus the bulk of your energies on completing projects and attaining goals.

Personal Year Number

	1	2	3	4	5	6	7	8	9
Jan	2	3	4	5	6	7	8	9	1
Feb	3	4	5	6	7	8	9	1	2
Mar	4	5	6	7	8	9	1	2	3
Apr	5	6	7	8	9	1	2	3	4
May	6	7	8	9	1	2	3	4	5
June	7	8	9	1	2	3	4	5	6
July	8	9	1	2	3	4	5	6	7
Aug	9	1	2	3	4	5	6	7	8
Sep	1	2	3	4	5	6	7	8	9
Oct	2	3	4	5	6	7	8	9	1
Nov	3	4	5	6	7	8	9	1	2
Dec	4	5	6	7	8	9	1	2	3

Note: Use the Personal Year number calculated in the previous exercise.

The Personal Month	A	B	C
Current Personal Year	_____	_____	_____
Calendar Month	_____	_____	_____
Sum of numbers in column C			_____
Reduce sum to single digit			_____

The Personal Day Number

For added insights on a day-to-day basis, consider your Personal Day number. This influence is less important than the Personal Month number, yet being aware of it can help with the planning and organizing of your weekly and daily activities. To calculate your Personal Day number, add the values—reduced to single digits or Master numbers—of your Personal Year, the Calendar Month, and Calendar Day. In the example below for February 14, for a person whose Personal Year is 7:

1. Personal Year number: 7.

2. Calendar Month: February, 2.

3. Calendar Day: 14 = 1 + 4 = 5.

4. Add the numbers: 7 + 2 + 5 = 14/5.

How to Calculate the Personal Day

Example for February 14 for a person whose Personal Year is 7.

	A	B	C
Current Personal Year	7	7	7
Calendar Month	2	2	2
Calendar Day	14	1+4	5
Sum of numbers in column C			14
Reduce sum to single digit		14/5	

The Personal Day number is 5 with a 14 influence.

In this example, there is a Karmic Debt number behind the Personal Day number, 14. If this was your number for this day and a friend had set you up on a dinner date, your Valentine's evening would probably not turn out as you expected! The 14/5 typically brings change, unexpected events, and surprises.

Calculate Your Personal Day

	A	B	C
Current Personal Year	_____	_____	_____
Calendar Month	_____	_____	_____
Calendar Day	_____	_____	_____
Sum of numbers in column C			_____
Reduce sum to single digit		_____	

Interpretations for Personal Days are similar to those for Personal Months and Personal Years, but should be scaled down to a day-to-day level of activity. Before interpreting a

Personal Day number, keep in mind your global yearly picture, that is, your Personal Year number, as well as your monthly trends as indicated by your Personal Month number. Also keep in mind your potential as indicated by your Life Path and Birth Day numbers, and your relationship to the numbers. Note Karmic Debt influences. The following interpretations are meant as suggestions to help you determine the nature of the energy of the day. Use the keywords to interpret your days according to your lifestyle.

1 (19/1) Personal Day

This is a good time to begin new activities, to look for a new job, or start a new project. You feel bold, confident, and ready to express initiative, take action, and get the gears in motion. This is your time. You could be feeling ambitious, creative, and energetic. You may be inclined to do things by yourself today. Beware of a tendency to see things from your point of view alone, ignoring the needs of others in the process. If a 19/1 Day, try not to be overly pushy with your plans. It isn't worth stepping on other people's toes to get what you want.

2 (11/2) Personal Day

Be receptive and wait for feedback from the world around you before making important decisions. Gather information, reach out, and touch base with leads and important contacts. Avoid conflict and misunderstandings. This is a good day for a romantic tête-à-tête. Pay particular attention to the needs of others. Even though you may tend to take things personally, try to remain tactful and diplomatic. Be a good listener, partner, or companion. You could be more tense, anxious, or sensitive than usual if this is an 11/2 Day.

3 Personal Day

This is a great day for scheduling social and fun events, dinner parties, and outings with friends. Focus on communications, return those phone calls you've been putting off, or work on a creative project. Schedule brainstorming sessions with colleagues or your team; work on your network of contacts. You may be feeling optimistic and positive, but could be a little disorganized or scattered today. Leave the day open; find avenues of creative self-expression. Have a good laugh, dress up, and enjoy a night on the town.

4 (13/4, 22/4) Personal Day

Apply yourself to the details of the day, stick to routine, and focus on the tasks at hand. Get rid of old projects that have been sitting on your desk, blocking progress in other areas of your work. Take care of accounting, bookkeeping, filing, or organizing your workspace. Spend time with family. Do household chores, home projects, renovations, or heavy physical work on a 4 Personal Day. If this is a 13/4 Day, you may be frustrated with the amount of work that seems to have piled up in front of you. If it is a 22/4 Day, you may feel pressed to get things accomplished.

5 (14/5) Personal Day

Expect changes to your plans, or unexpected or surprise occurrences. This is a good day for adventure, new experiences, and travel, and for promoting yourself or expanding your business. You won't be very interested in doing paperwork and tedious activities today. Give yourself a little room to breathe. Be flexible. If a 14/5, don't expect things to go as planned; the day is likely to be more hectic than you would like. Expect surprises or upsets. Guard against a tendency to be impatient, to overindulge in food and drink, or to avoid responsibility.

6 Personal Day

Take care of family business and pay attention to loved ones today. You will need to establish some measure of balance in your life after yesterday's hectic pace. Demands will be made on your time and energy, and you will be very much appreciated as you tend to your responsibilities. Let people know that you really care. If you can make some time for a creative project, you will feel more in harmony with yourself. Plan a romantic dinner, a family gathering, a relaxing massage, a movie, or a visit to an art gallery.

7 (16/7) Personal Day

You may feel inclined to take some quiet time out for yourself. Reflect, meditate, read, or take a spa day. This is a good time for intellectual activities, research, and study. Avoid excessive stress and confrontation. Do some serious thinking; review your monthly plan. Go for a long walk in the woods, listen to music, spend some quiet time in the garden, or on a hobby. This isn't a good day for planning a social event. If a 16/7 Day, avoid confrontations in personal relationships. You are not likely to be feeling warm and affectionate. You could take things personally or feel misunderstood.

8 Personal Day

Deal with money and power issues now. This is a good day for finances, business, shopping, or making important purchases. You are feeling empowered, driven to achieve your goals, maybe even fearless, and at the top of your game. Schedule that important business meeting, or make business decisions. Your confidence level is high, and you believe in your ability to achieve your goals. It's time to show what you're made of.

9 Personal Day

Finish off projects, clean up your office or home, and try to unwind. Clear up loose ends. This is not the time to start new projects or to commit to long-term plans. Spend a day outdoors, enjoying nature, go for a drive in the country, or take in an art show or exhibition. Get some rest. Do something for others; participate in a community event or fundraiser. Follow up on messages and phone calls; have lunch with friends. Release all grievances and anxieties. Be generous. Give of yourself. This is a good day for a public appearance.

Exercise: Key Life Sectors

In preparation for using the knowledge of the numbers effectively, it is important that you know where and how to invest your time and energy. The following exercise is one I use to help clients identify Key Life Sectors, those areas of life that you feel are important, based on your values, in which you feel you should be devoting time and energy. It is similar to the Identifying Roles approach used by Stephen Covey in his Habit 3: Putting First Things First.[2] As an aid to defining your Key Life Sectors, consider the following questions. Then, list your Key Life Sectors.

- What is most important in my life?

- What do I value the most?

- If I could do only one thing in my life, what would that be?

---

2. Stephen R. Covey, *The 7 Habits of Highly Effective People* (New York: Fireside, 1990), 162–63.

- What can I not live without?

- What do I need more of in my life?

- What did I dream of doing when I was young?

- What makes me smile?

- What gives me energy?

- What am I passionate about?

- What do I love to talk about with friends?

- What makes me jump out of bed in the morning?

- How would I like to spend my time?

- What do I believe I should be working on?

- Where do I feel the most useful to others?

- When am I the most appreciated by others?

- What is that one thing I would do if only I had time?

- What do I plan to do when I retire?

- What do I want to do more of?

Look for patterns in your answers. If you consistently answered that you would like to have more fun at work, at home, when you retire, one day when you have more time, or that when you were young you dreamed of being an entertainer, then perhaps you have a deep and unanswered need for lightening up a bit and should consider finding an outlet for self-expression. You may have a long-buried number 3 influence somewhere, the number of the arts and entertainment. Take this need seriously, so to speak, and make time for an activity that would allow it in your life—if not on a daily basis, then at least on a weekly basis. You might consider joining an improv group or community theater.

Some example Key Life Sectors:

- Self/personal development

- Family, spouse, parents

- Friends, social activities

- Health, fitness

- Boss, manager, employee

- Business development

- Professional development, career

- Creativity, self-expression

- Community involvement/sharing

- Home projects

- Fun time

Make a list of the five or six Key Life Sectors that are most important to you. These are the areas of life in which you will be devoting time and energy. Try to establish a healthy balance between the personal and professional sectors. Sometimes, simply reestablishing equilibrium in your life is sufficient to release much accumulated stress.

My Key Life Sectors
1
2
3
4
5
6

Be reasonable in your choice of areas of activity. Choosing too many areas of focus can lead to failure, as you will be less likely to meet your objectives. It is best to focus on fewer areas for now, adding to your list later, as you master your time and ability to plan. You cannot do it all at the same time. Accept this fact and you will find much stress magically disappear! Also, your list of Key Life Sectors will change as the demands of your life and your lifestyle change. By remaining open and flexible, you will always be doing the things you feel are right for you at any given moment.

Exercise: My Personal History

Another very interesting exercise that you will find most helpful is to go back in time and review the events of your life as though it were a movie. Make a list, year by year, if you can, of not only the important events, but also the quiet times, the apparently insignificant periods of your life. Calculate the Personal Year numbers for those years that contain important events, such as a move, the start of a job, the end of a job, the start and end of school, or the start or end of an important relationship. You will probably identify recurring cycles in your life. This exercise will give you an excellent idea of what to expect the next time a particular Personal Year comes around. If you are a 3 Life Path, for example, you may find that 6 Personal Years have been very productive times for creative activities. From this exercise, you may identify relationship trends, financial trends, or career trends. Refer to your Personal History as you read the descriptions of the Personal Years in the following chapters.

Events of My Life			
Date	Age	PY*	Event

*Personal Year

FOUR

Renewal, New Beginnings, Rebirth

THE 1 PERSONAL YEAR

✳

1	2	3	4	5	6	7	8	9

The 1 Personal Year is a time of new beginnings, a time for making adjustments to your life journey, especially if you feel that you have been led off course. This could be an important crossroads. It is a key year in that it is the one time when you can effectively break away from the past and set your life in a completely new direction. Now is the time to abandon old patterns and launch those new projects you've been dreaming of and planning for so long. If you are in a position that is right for you, a field that allows you to grow and develop your personal potential, this will be the ideal time to take the next big step forward.

Make the adjustments in your personal and professional life that will eventually enable you to pursue those activities that most closely reflect your values and goals. If you are in a job or situation that you dislike or that does not allow you to grow as you would like, then this may be the time to make some changes. You can now steer yourself in a new area of activity, if this is what is required to make your life more fulfilling. The 1 Personal Year allows you to make radical changes and break from the past.

Note your response to the "My Experience of the Number 1" exercise from chapter 1. How you relate to this energy will in part determine your experience of the 1 Personal

Year. Autonomy, independence, self-reliance, initiative, and a strong sense of self will contribute to the success of your new endeavors. This is the time to take care of *you*. Focus on your life purpose, your values, your desires, and your goals. If in the past you have been shy, inhibited, reserved, or reluctant to take advantage of opportunities for advancement, you may try being more assertive and bold now. New opportunities are likely to open up. You could be offered a position in an entirely different field of work, or you may have an opening in a new location. Significant life transitions are common in a 1 Personal Year.

Reevaluate your long-term plan, personally and professionally. If you haven't defined one yet, now would be the time to do so. Consider projects that could take a few years to complete. You have time on your side now. There is less pressure to reach your goals now as you are just at the beginning of the cycle. This is the time to transform your dreams, aspirations, hopes, and intentions into reality. It is time to take action. A positive attitude and a bit of courage will help you overcome the obstacles that have previously prevented you from making significant changes in your life. Be bold and confident.

Embrace change and adventure. Move forward with fresh, new, and innovative ideas. More importantly, address the challenges of your particular Life Path. Take initiative and practice healthy assertiveness while maintaining respect for others. This is your key to success for the entire year. If you are ready to retire or reduce your workload, again, this is the time to set the new pace. It is up to you to carve out a path with a new future for yourself.

You may already be engaged in activities that reflect well your talents and abilities, and feel no need to make major adjustments at this time in your life. It is not necessary to change your direction each time you reach a 1 Personal Year. However, it is important to undertake something new in a 1 Personal Year, even if it doesn't lead to any major professional or career changes. Learning something new can be both invigorating and empowering. Undertaking new activities prevents you from becoming overly entrenched in old ways of doing things, opens up your creative energies, gives added confidence, and facilitates progress. Tackling new challenges and opportunities favors flexibility, which makes it easier to make changes and adjustments as they arise.

During a 1 Personal Year, it is not uncommon to feel alone, sometimes lost or unsupported, unsure about whether or not you are doing the right thing. It can be frightening to face the future with little reassurance or guarantee that your projects will work out. Practice tuning into your intuition; be open to receiving inner guidance. People in your immediate environment may feel threatened as you begin to move in a new direction. Others will not always agree with your new ideas and plans, and may not be supportive as you move forward with your life. Most people resist change. The old "if it ain't broke, don't fix it" approach is rather well entrenched in our way of thinking.

Sometimes change can be interpreted as a signal that something was previously wrong, inadequate, or somehow unsatisfactory. Often, this is actually the case. When a person suddenly makes a decision to move in an entirely new direction, those who are close may wonder if they have done something wrong. Your decision for change may cause them to question their own way of doing things. Change can be unsettling, even threatening. The best policy is to make certain that your decision is based on your inner guidance, and to not make excuses or elaborate reasons for your decision to others. People will eventually accept your choices when they see that you are in a far better place for it. They may even support you in your endeavors at a later date. Everyone loves a champion, and following the voice of your heart will allow you to be the champion of your life.

At the same time, be mindful of those people in your life who may feel neglected as you focus on yourself this year. Keep the lines of communication open. Reassure loved ones that you will not abandon them. Share your ideas and impressions with the special few who are there to support you during times of change and transition.

Natalie, a 19/1 Life Path, began to dance at the age of 3½. In her mid-teens, a doctor informed her that her hip joints and knees were permanently damaged, and that she should consider other career alternatives. Devastated, she cried for months. But in typical 1 Life Path fashion, she pulled herself up and declared that she would rather try and fail than to never have given herself a chance. She graduated from high school in a special dance program in the spring of a 9 Personal Year. In the fall of that same year, she began her first session at college, but for some strange reason, was compelled to enroll in the pure and applied science program. In a 9 Personal Year, as you will see in chapter 12, it's not uncommon to become distracted and veer off track. "If ever I need these courses," she reasoned, "I'll have them."

The following January, now in a 1 Personal Year, at the start of a new epicycle, she switched out of pure and applied science and moved to communications, making the adjustment toward a more appropriate direction, given her lifelong interest in dance. (Note that there was no dance program at her college, otherwise this would have been her choice.) By the end of that epicycle, Natalie had successfully completed college, obtained a Bachelor of Fine Arts in contemporary dance at university and a postgraduate degree in fine arts management, completed a series of certificates in Pilates training, and established a successful business as a freelance dance teacher and Pilates instructor. The following year, a 1 Personal Year, she began developing ideas for a new approach that would integrate dance and Pilates. If you aren't exhausted just reading this, keep in mind that all the while, she worked two to three part-time jobs to pay for school and rent! Natalie's journey reflects well the drive, energy, initiative, creativity, and autonomy of the 19/1 Life Path.

For some people, especially those needing a significant life makeover, things don't always become clear until the later months, September or October, of the 1 Personal Year. Don't panic if you haven't gotten a clear picture of your life direction on the first day of January. At the same time, it is important to take some initiative in a 1 Personal Year, so as to engage the energy of the new epicycle. Even if things are still unclear by the end of the year, do try something new, even if it is only a small step. Also keep in mind that it can take the first two to three years of the new epicycle before all your changes and new projects can fully take shape.

Don, the president of an IT company, stretched his wings the year he turned fifty, a 1 Personal Year. A typical 13/4 Life Path, he had dedicated the better part of his years to family and career. A few years before, he had purchased a motorcycle, which he enjoyed riding to and from the office and other short distances. True to his cautious, reliable, and dependable 4 Life Path, Don had never been much of a risk taker. That year, with the children grown up and the company well established, he felt confident enough to venture out into the world. He joined a local motorcycle club and signed on for a 2,200-mile, ten-day ride to the East Coast. This was a challenging trek for a novice rider, but fuelled by his fresh new 1 Personal Year energy, he was ready.

You miss 100% of the shots you never take.

WAYNE GRETZKY

Note that when you reach a Personal Year that has the same numerical value as your Life Path number, this can be a very significant time of life. It is as though your Life Path number becomes supercharged, and its energy needs to manifest itself in an urgent manner. If you have not mastered this number, or are expressing negative aspects of it, these negative traits may be exaggerated at this time. Additional self-awareness is helpful during these intense periods. In Natalie's case, her 19/1 Life Path energy becomes highly activated in a 1 Personal Year. At the time she entered college, she also began a new relationship. Barely a couple of days into the following 1 Personal Year, to her chagrin, she ended the relationship. The intensity of the 1 energy did not lend itself well to resolving relationship issues at that time of her life, and in true 1 fashion, she chose to forge ahead on her own.

In a 1 Personal Year, keep in mind that you are at the beginning of a new cycle. It can take up to two years before the energy of change is fully manifested and takes its place in your life. Do not expect results to happen right away; you have the next several years to develop your projects. You may need to exercise a little patience, especially if you have quick-minded and quick-acting numbers like the 1 and the 5 among your core numbers.

The 1 Personal Year Month by Month

Note that the following descriptions for the Personal Months are to be used as guidelines for determining possible scenarios. Use the keywords from chapter 1 to interpret potential trends that apply to your particular lifestyle. Each person is unique, and each has a unique relationship with the numbers. Also keep in mind that the Personal Month trends are secondary to the Personal Year trends, and should be considered along with your Life Path and Birth Date numbers as well as your current Personal Year number.

JANUARY (2 Personal Month): Receptivity, New Beginnings

On the heels of a 9 Personal Year, the 1 Personal Year can be an exciting time, with new perspectives and a renewed sense of vigor and energy. You may still be reeling from the emotional intensity and fatigue of your recently ended epicycle, but expectations for the future are starting to grow. You may need to deal with relationship issues as you embark on a new long-term cycle. Use diplomacy and tact in dealing with others. Study any new plans or ideas that came up at the end of last year. Take the time to allow things to fall into place. There is no need to rush now. Clear up any loose ends remaining from last year. Pay attention to feedback from the universe around you. If you are experiencing any doubts about your new direction, examine their origins for validity. Change can cause fear and uncertainty, and a 1 Personal Year is often a year of big changes.

FEBRUARY (3 Personal Month): Creativity, Optimism

You are probably going to be feeling much more optimistic this month; in fact, you are ready to take on the world. Your creative energies are beginning to flow as you start to realize that a new cycle has effectively begun. Imagination, which may have lain dormant for some time now, is reawakened and new ideas start to rise to the surface. You express yourself well and are open to new opportunities. You feel lucky and hopeful, ready to take on your new life. Take advantage of your social contacts as you begin to leave the past behind and start on your new journey. Romance is in the air. Explore your options, but take the time to think things through.

MARCH (4 Personal Month): Organization, Work

Now is the time to buckle down and concentrate on your new projects and goals. This is a foundation month, and your ability to work hard and pay attention to details will determine whether or not your projects will get off to a strong start. You may need to get yourself focused and organized, especially if last month you allowed yourself to become distracted. Begin to build a powerful and effective plan for your goals. If you are well organized, you will feel less restricted as you get down to work. You are very productive now and much can be accomplished. You may have to give up some of your social time to pull this off. Fear not, growth follows shortly. Don't ignore those home projects; make time for family.

APRIL (5 Personal Month): Adventure, the Unexpected

If you have started off with a solid foundation, the new opportunities presented this month will contribute nicely to the growth and expansion of your projects. Travel is possible. Unusual or unique opportunities may arise. This is a time of adventure and excitement. Approach new opportunities with an open mind and one foot on the ground. This is a good time to promote yourself and your business, applying some of those new ideas and approaches that have been stirring, waiting for an opportunity to be expressed. Stick to your plan if you don't want to veer off course. Leave some free time in your schedule; you will need a little freedom this month.

MAY (6 Personal Month): Balance, Harmony

If you are involved in a service-related industry, changes and new approaches may be tried out now. Tend to responsibilities. You will need to maintain balance between your work and personal life, keeping loved ones informed of your new direction, projects, and ideas. Others may feel insecure as you proceed with new plans this year. Let family and friends know that you will not be leaving them behind. If there are unexpressed issues in your personal relationships, try to bring them out with sensitivity and compassion. In all matters, remain true to your values.

JUNE (7 Personal Month): Reflection, Analysis

Career moves to the back burner as you pause to think things through. Are your goals clear? Do you see your path clearly before you? Review your planning and goal setting for the year and make adjustments as necessary. Take some quiet time out, meditate, practice yoga, or read a book. Also, do any background work, study, or research that may help ensure the accomplishment of your goals. This is a time of learning, understanding, depth, and insight. Yet, try to keep a balance between your inner focus and your personal relationships. Avoid selfishly excluding loved ones. Instead, simply let them know that you need a little quiet time.

JULY (8 Personal Month): Plans Consolidated, Accomplishment

July is a power month in a year of new beginnings. This is a great time to get your projects moving forward or to expand your career or business activities. You should start to experience some progress now as the energy of your new epicycle becomes fully engaged. Your focus this month should be on career and finances. This can be a profitable month as business and financial activities take on more importance. You are in a good position to reap the rewards of the efforts of the past few months. Important new business relationships may be started now. If you must take your vacation this month, you might find it difficult to take your mind off business. If you can, schedule your vacation for next month or November.

AUGUST (9 Personal Month): Release, Completion

You will find it easy to bring your plans to completion this month. Whatever was holding you back can be easily released now. Be willing to let go of restrictions, old habits, outdated relationships, and behaviors. Free yourself of any remaining obstacles and blockages to progress, any issues that may remain from last year, a 9 Personal Year. You may also choose to let go of some of the least appropriate new ideas you came up with this year. Focus on a positive attitude, and avoid being consumed by fear or feelings of loss. Look forward, not backward. Your new cycle will be completely set in motion next month. Leave your comfort zone, go out, extend, and stretch yourself. Volunteer in your community; do something for others. Travel.

SEPTEMBER (1 Personal Month): Action, Initiative

Expect much movement and energy this month. Step it up and get ready to manifest! Be bold, be daring. Express your uniqueness, your creativity, and your leadership ability. Leave all fears behind. Begin a new lifestyle, plan a new business, start a health regimen, begin a workout program, or join a gym. This is your chance to steer your life in a new direction, where you can really make important changes, or if necessary, a fresh new start. A new relationship could be burgeoning; next month you will know whether or not you wish to pursue it. Make sure the actions you undertake reflect your long-term direction and goals. Focus on yourself, your needs, and your desires without being overly selfish. Avoid alienating others. Begin to take those important steps that will lead you substantially closer to your goals.

OCTOBER (2 Personal Month): Patience, Receptivity

The pace slows down a bit this month, so you'll need to be patient. The new projects you started will take time to develop and take shape. Pay attention to details. Keep an open mind, and be receptive to external feedback as well as to inner guidance. Others may provide valuable input, contributing in a positive way to the growth of your ideas and projects. Cooperation could be of benefit. You are more sensitive and intuitive than usual and may take things to heart. A new romance could bloom now. If you have a partner, stir up the romance in your relationship. Take the time to catch your breath and reestablish a sense of peace and harmony. Reconnect with those who are close to you. Your next Personal Year, a 2, will bring relationships to the fore.

NOVEMBER (3 Personal Month): Enthusiasm, Joie de Vivre

New projects are well underway by now, so you can relax a little and enjoy life. A positive, enthusiastic attitude will move you forward and inspire others to join with you. You feel as though you are on top of the world and your optimism is contagious. Be careful not to become too distracted or to scatter your energies. With an endless stream of new ideas rising to the surface, you may find it difficult to focus on your goals and your work. It is more difficult to remain disciplined this month; there are just too many fun things to do, too many social events, dinner parties, and other distractions. Do take the time to enjoy the company of friends while maintaining a focus on your goals.

DECEMBER (4 Personal Month): Work, Work, Work

Like March, December is a time to reestablish structure and organization in your life, but now that your new cycle is well established, you will want to focus your energies on strengthening your foundation. Try to incorporate some of those great ideas you had last month into your daily activities. It will make your work seem less dreary. You will need to pay attention to details, order, and routine. Home and family may also require your attention. If you get yourself organized, things will go more smoothly. Although progress will at times appear to be slow, your efforts and dedication will pay off in the long run. Hang in there. Check your work habits and day-to-day routine for efficiency; eliminate time wasters.

The 1 Personal Year Workshop

Complete this workshop at the beginning of the year along with your yearly planning and goal setting.

1. Relative to your Life Path, Birth Day number, and personal experience of the number 1, how do you feel about new beginnings? Do you have difficulty being autonomous and taking initiative? Are you comfortable starting new projects? If you are lacking in autonomy and confidence, look for support from a coach or friend while you attempt to make changes in your life.

2. Recall the last time you experienced a 1 Personal Year. (See the "My Personal History" exercise in chapter 3.) What new activities did you begin? What significant changes did you make at the time? If everything remained the same as in previous

years, that is, if you did not make any changes, was it because your life was right on track or because you were fearful of change? Over the years that followed your last 1 Personal Year, did you reach your goals?

3. Relative to where you are now, what new element(s) do you need to integrate into your life? For example, if you have an 8 Life Path and haven't yet manifested your full power potential, this would be a good time to take a first step. What one activity could you do that would help you integrate your personal power? If you have a 2 Life Path and haven't yet overcome your codependency issues, what one thing could you do to improve or heal this situation? What activity could you undertake that would help you develop self-reliance? Now would be a good time to begin that special project or activity that has for too long been relegated to the "one day when . . ." pile.

4. Review your Key Life Sectors list. (See "Exercise: Key Life Sectors" in chapter 3.) Are all these sectors relevant in your life at this time? Remove old sectors, and add new ones based on the new direction you are choosing for yourself now.

5. Find one new activity or goal to be accomplished this year for each of your Key Life Sectors. Bringing new elements into your life will invigorate you in many ways. Establish new goals for yourself in each sector. For example, you may want to increase your sales quota over last year's by 20% or lose thirty pounds and find a way to keep it off. Set specific, measurable goals. Determine a plan for the achievement of these goals. March and December of the 1 Personal Year—4 Personal Months—are excellent months to work on your plans. Be realistic in determining your objectives for the year. Setting unrealistic expectations or goals is more likely to lead to failure.

6. Toxic relationships are as harmful as bad habits. Move away from harmful or outdated relationships. People will not always agree with your new ideas and plans, and may not be supportive as you move forward with your life.

Exercise: Year-End Review

Complete this exercise at the end of your 1 Personal Year.

1. What new directions did your life take this year? In what areas did you express increased initiative, self-reliance, and courage?

2. What are the benefits of these changes?

3. What is the most important lesson you learned this year?

4. What new knowledge will you bring into your upcoming 2 Personal Year?

The 1 Personal Year Goal Setting and Planning Worksheet

As an aid to your yearly planning exercise, complete the following worksheet. Set goals for each of your current Key Life Sectors. This year could bring considerable opportunities for change. Now is the time to set your life in a new direction. Your goals should reflect your values and desires at this time of your life.

Goal Setting and Planning Worksheet My 1 Personal Year Renewal, New Beginnings, Rebirth	
Key Life Sectors	*Goals for the year*
1	i
	ii
	iii
2	i
	ii
	iii
3	i
	ii
	iii
4	i
	ii
	iii
5	i
	ii
	iii
6	i
	ii
	iii

FIVE

Cooperation, Receptivity, Adaptability

THE 2 PERSONAL YEAR

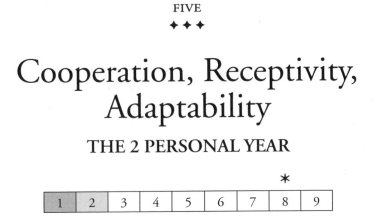

The energy of the 1 divides, separates, and projects itself outward until the 1 becomes 2. This establishes a climate of duality: myself and others, action and response, inner and outer, dynamic and static. That which manifested from the core of the self in the 1 Personal Year, must now find its proper place and form outside itself. Having become 2, the 1 is now polarized. This can create tension, both within and without. Wherein the last year there was a sense of limitless possibilities, now boundaries, obstacles, and limitations are beginning to appear.

It is not uncommon to experience feelings of frustration and impatience in a 2 Personal Year. This is a time for cooperation and receptivity. Yet, as much as you need to be cooperative at this stage of your development, you may be overly sensitive to the input of others, even resentful of the meddling and intrusion of outside forces. The new projects and activities you began last year are still vulnerable, in their early stages of development.

You realize now that you are not alone. You can either do battle against perceived external obstacles, or learn to work with them. You may benefit by taking advantage of the resources available outside yourself. Depending on your ability to cooperate and work with others, you will either thrive with the help and support of others or suffer the frustration of having to share, to be open to the ideas of others, and to make compromises. If you are a 1, 5, or 8 Life Path, you may experience some impatience with the need to wait for the input of others to move forward with your projects.

While the 2 Personal Year may bring you face-to-face with the responses from the world outside yourself, it will also bring out your inner reactions to the initiatives that you undertook in your 1 Personal Year. This is where you may encounter insecurities, fears, or doubts about your newly formed projects or ideas. If you are prone to doubting and second-guessing yourself, you may have to struggle hard at this time to maintain sufficient focus on your goals.

The universe may show you alternate routes or different ways of approaching your new projects. By maintaining an open mind and being receptive to your environment, you can gain valuable insights about your direction and purpose. With this additional information, you can make the necessary changes and adjustments that will allow you to be more successful in the long term.

This is a time of increased interaction with others, and you may feel more vulnerable or emotional than usual. You are likely to face a variety of relationship issues, not just personal, but also social, business, and professional. You will be dealing with perceptions that will have to be reconciled, viewpoints that must be discussed, and future plans that will require adjustments, cooperation, and fine-tuning.

Be patient, observant, and receptive. You will be better prepared. Choose a course of action that reflects your inner desire, rather than one designed to accommodate your fears or insecurities. If you are a people-pleaser, beware of doing things just to make someone else happy, while ignoring your own goals in the process. Take your time in making decisions. If necessary, seek guidance or counseling; get help to deal with challenges or blockages. Take the time to meditate, study, plan, and assimilate the energies at work in your life. Your epicycle is young and just beginning to take shape. Take the time you need to establish yourself firmly.

The 2 Personal Year brings out all forms of interaction with others, and often requires that you be flexible, cooperative, and adaptable, and that you make adjustments as necessary. It favors contacts, associations, and relationships with women in particular. It is important to think of others, not only of yourself during this time. As this is a relational year during which you are probably adjusting to new directions, remember to be mindful of the impact of your actions on loved ones. Be tactful and sensitive. This can be a period of stress in your encounters with others, especially if difficulties and unexpressed grievances have been building up. Good communication skills, patience, and understanding will help you reconcile your differences.

The 2 Personal Year is an excellent time to seek professional help such as counseling, coaching, therapy, or mentoring. Positive, constructive support at this early and often delicate time of the new epicycle can be very productive. At the same time, it is important to be discerning in your choice of confidants. In the early stages of your epicycle, you may be vulnerable to the negative opinions of others. A cynical comment can quickly take the wind out of your sails and stop you in your progress.

Robert, a CMA with a history of failed relationships and too many career changes, decided to take matters in hand. In his 2 Personal Year, he undertook a process with a therapist to uncover the reasons for the failure of his relationships. He also hired a personal coach to help him define a clear career path. These steps gave him the tools and the confidence he needed to approach these important aspects of his life in a healthy manner. He admitted that this is not something that he would normally have done, but it seemed fitting at that particular time of his life. The counseling and the coaching gave him the clarity and direction he needed to set himself on track.

Phase II Thinking

We are all familiar with the exhilarating energy of the number 1. It begins with a great idea. Excitedly, you discuss it with a close friend. Anything is possible in this initial phase; no obstacle is so great that it couldn't possibly be dealt with. You suddenly feel clever, inspired, and invigorated as new life flows through your veins. You experience joy and confidence; nothing can stop you. Your entire existence has new meaning. You begin to plan and speculate; you imagine what it will be like and how you will feel once you have achieved your brand-new goal.

What almost inevitably follows this exciting new beginning is the reaction phase. The 2 is defined as the number of receptivity, emotional response, and sensitivity to others and to environmental factors. While the 1 represents all that is pure yang (pure male energy), the 2 is pure yin (pure female energy), geared toward survival rather than toward adventure. The 2 is inward-focused; the 1 is outward-focused. It is emotional and intuitive rather than rational, reactive and receptive rather than proactive and dynamic.

Even if it isn't one of your core numbers, you will regularly experience the energy of the number 2, because it naturally follows the 1. Whenever you experience a beginning, you will experience a reaction.

Typically, the day following the manifestation of your brilliant new idea, you will encounter the reaction phase, or the doubting phase. This is where you face the inner dialogue, often manifesting as various forms of resistance: *I couldn't possibly do that . . . What a dumb idea . . . What was I thinking? It's too much work . . . I don't have what it takes . . . It would take too long . . . I don't have the time . . . I don't have the money . . . My partner would never go for it. . . .* I call it the Backtalk. Suddenly, the list of reasons for not following through with your new idea grows longer than the list of reasons why you should pursue it. The initial enthusiasm begins to wane. Discouragement, fear, and disappointment drown out passion and optimism. Exhilaration quickly fades, and the next thing you know, another great idea is abandoned and returned to the realm of the formless, unrealized potential.

Recognize the pattern? I call it Phase II Thinking, the reaction. This is a hurdle many people encounter when undergoing a process of personal growth and transformation. Most people have experienced it, to greater or lesser degrees, at least a few times in their lives. However, each time you succumb to the negative dialogue of the 2 energy, you re-inforce a pattern of failure, leaving behind a trail of faltering hopes and missed opportunities. Sometimes, it is better to make an honest attempt and fail, rather than not make any attempt at all. Very often, it is in the learning obtained while attempting something, even if it leads to failure, that we gain the knowledge, or the keys required for reaching subsequent successes.

The 2 Personal Year needn't automatically lead to dead ends, or prevent you from fulfilling your dreams. The key to managing Phase II Thinking is to not allow yourself to remain locked in its negative processes. A certain amount of caution, reflection, and analysis is good. But first take your idea, study it in terms of desirability and feasibility, then look at the obstacles as well as the potential benefits of finding solutions and pursuing its full development. Phase II is natural and even necessary. It calls on discernment. If you didn't take the time to go through it, you would constantly be throwing yourself in the direction of any and every idea that came your way, and in the end, little would be accomplished.

Relinquishing Family Grievances

A 2 Year is often a time for love and romance. If you began a new relationship last year, it may grow to the next level this year. Marriage is common in a 2 Personal Year. Feeling more emotional and vulnerable than normal, you may seek the support, affection, and protection of someone close. There is a need to share. The following is adapted from a feature article published in my online newsletter, *Success Matters*. It sums up my experience of a very important 2 Personal Year and is included here as inspiration for those who might be looking for an enjoyable way to deepen their relationships or reconnect with family members.

Throughout most of October, the Sun joins Jupiter in the sign of Libra, a cardinal air sign, ruled by Venus, the planet of love, values, and relationships. It is the sign of social interaction, marriage, and partnerships of all kinds. Librans love to talk, discuss, debate, and chat on a variety of topics, in various environments. Rare is the Libran who has nothing to say on a subject, no matter how shy or reclusive he may be.

My dad, with his Libra Moon, was no exception. He loved family gatherings . . . Christmas, Easter, grandchildren's birthdays . . . he was there. As a Taurus, also a Venus-ruled sign, he was quite the gourmet or, I should say more precisely, *gourmand!* On October 17, the day of the lunar eclipse, it will have been six months since my father passed away. Much has happened in our lives since then. It has been a period of adjustment for all of us—parents, children, and grandchildren alike—as we scrambled to fill the gap left behind by his unexpected departure. Without a plan or script to follow, we somehow managed to pull together, being there for each other whenever the need arose, no questions asked. Pulling together was the natural thing to do.

In my consultation work, and also socially, I often hear people complain about their families: parents, in-laws, children, siblings . . . the list of complaints is long and often quite colorful. Family ties are easily taken for granted in a time when a family can be easily destroyed simply by being in the wrong place on the planet at the wrong time. In our family, May has always been a month of celebrations, with the birthdays of my daughters, my nephew, and my dad. And then there's Mother's Day, Victoria Day, and Father's Day—plenty of opportunities for dinners and the first barbecues of summer. For us, this summer's dinner schedule was conspicuously meager.

Alone now, with my daughters living far across town, I decided to institute Sunday family dinners, something I had wanted to do for years. Cooking and experimenting with cuisines from around the world is a pleasure I share with the girls, and when Caroline mentioned that she missed my home cooking, it didn't take much for me to set my plan in motion. I'd been craving a good homemade Moroccan couscous. Couscous was way too much food for one person, even two people. So this would be my first dinner. I let the word out that I would be making a couscous on the first Sunday of August. Cook it and they will come, I thought cleverly. . . .

And they came . . . my daughters and their friends and my mom and one of my brothers . . . and we had a lovely time and a real hoot playing the Dictionary Game. This was our first gathering since my dad's passing. The following month, four more members added themselves to my family dinner as my other brother and his wife joined in for a night of sushi and sake. Although my dinners have since toggled between Saturdays and Sundays, adjusted to suit everyone's schedules (a wonderful number 2 trait), they have become a monthly event for our family. Everyone participates, enthusiastically searching the Internet and cookbooks for unique recipe ideas and cultural tidbits and anecdotes. We have since feasted on a variety of cuisines from around the world, with theme menus planned months in advance, including country French cuisine, Nova Scotia seafood, Szechwan, traditional Greek fare, the cuisine of Brazil, Thailand, California, Mexico, down-home Quebec, and a Passover Seder thrown in for good measure.

A true gastronome, my dad would have loved these gatherings. Now, when we get together for dinner, I feel as though he is right there, watching over us, smiling, pleased that we have moved on, relieved that we have taken care of each other and that my mom is okay and we are looking out for each other. In a way, these dinners are a tribute to his memory.

The next time you feel yourself projecting a grievance toward a family member, perhaps you might want to consider the impermanence of the world in which we live. And in that moment between thought and action, that special instant in which you are free to choose, you might consider relinquishing your grievance and choosing love instead. Holding a grievance will not make you feel any better, but choosing love absolutely will.

The 2 Personal Year Month by Month

Note that the following descriptions for the Personal Months are to be used as guidelines for determining possible scenarios. Use the keywords from chapter 1 to interpret potential trends that apply to your particular lifestyle. Each person is unique, and each has a unique relationship with the numbers. Also keep in mind that the Personal Month trends are secondary to the Personal Year trends, and should be considered along with your Life Path and Birth Date numbers as well as your current Personal Year number.

JANUARY (3 Personal Month): Social Life, Romance

What a great way to start the new year! The energy and optimism of the number 3 is always a welcome influence. Although social contacts are emphasized now, keep in mind that as this is a 2 Personal Year, you would do well to keep some of your new ideas and plans to yourself. You are still in a process of inner change and growth, therefore vulnerable to the influence of others. Be discriminating in your choice of confidants. What you need now, above all else, is the support of a positive ally. Surround yourself with optimistic and success-minded individuals. Romance is in the air. If single, you could meet someone who strikes your fancy; if you are in a relationship, spice it up a little, go somewhere exotic.

FEBRUARY (4 Personal Month): Work, Focus, Cooperation

As with all 4 Personal Months, you will need to focus on details and hard work. Get family members involved in a home renovation project you've been putting off, or help your mother reorganize her attic. Your dedication and earnestness are inspiring, but remember to remain attentive to other people's ideas as you dive into the task at hand. Although you are keen in getting the job done, be cooperative, diplomatic, and delicate. The pace might be slow, but measurable progress can be made. Learning to work in harmony with others is part of the lesson in a 2 Personal Year. Attend to money and financial matters; delay the purchase of expensive items for a better time.

MARCH (5 Personal Month): Opportunities, Travel, Surprises

You will need to be extra flexible this month, as unexpected circumstances come into play. Avoid risky ventures and stay away from get-rich-quick schemes. If it looks too good to be true, it probably is. This could be an adventurous and exciting month. Use innovative approaches to promote yourself or to market your services. Try to do things a little differently. Opportunities may present themselves as you meet new people. Think twice before turning your back on a relationship that appears to have grown old with time. Remain rational and don't lose your focus. Unless you are actively seeking romance, beware of idle flirtations. Do something fun and exciting with your partner. A 2 Personal Year is one of slow growth.

APRIL (6 Personal Month): Measure, Family, Service

You may have the opportunity to reconnect with an old acquaintance, or a relationship that has served its time could be reevaluated or even come to an end. Friends, coworkers, or family members need your help more than usual. Responsibilities at work are also on the rise, and your ability to deal with situations in a harmonious and peaceful manner will leave you in good stead with your employers. Use diplomacy and sensitivity in delicate or difficult situations. Arrange a romantic getaway with your special partner. You need balance to be productive; review your weekly calendar and make sure you haven't been led off course. Your people skills will either be tested or put to good use.

MAY (7 Personal Month): Reflection, Intuition, Reserve

Plan a quiet, peaceful vacation or some time by yourself, even if it's just to sort through an old CD collection or clean out your garage. Study, do some research, explore a deeper aspect of yourself, your work, or your craft. You may want to examine the new plans you made last year and make any adjustments, based on what you have learned to date this year. Remember, a 2 Personal Year is a time to be receptive. Study the messages you've been given; look for guidance. Don't force yourself to produce visible results now. Be sensitive to close ones while you become introspective. Let them know you need a little time by yourself, reassure them that you are not pulling away on a permanent basis. This is not a good month for planning big social events.

JUNE (8 Personal Month): Power, Negotiation, Accomplishment

The relationships you have cultivated so far this year are starting to bear fruit. This is a time of much activity and progress in joint projects. Maintain an unhurried pace in all endeavors. Your plans are starting to take shape, and you are probably feeling much more confident than you have over the past couple of months. Use your power to negotiate a gain, but do so in a diplomatic way. Career advancement is possible now. This is a good time to handle financial affairs. Avoid becoming drawn into a power struggle. Look for harmonious solutions in all situations. Your focus is on career rather than on romance.

JULY (9 Personal Month): Completion, Release, Endings

Even though you are feeling that progress has been slow this year, finishing off certain aspects of your projects this month will give you a sense of accomplishment. A special relationship may come to an end. This can be an emotional time, as you let go of outdated ties, habits, or activities. You could be experiencing doubt and uncertainty. Pursue an activity that revolves around helping others; volunteer in your community. This will help deflate any pent-up emotions you may be feeling as a result of releasing the past. Do something healing, spend time outdoors, schedule a spa weekend. This is a month of endings; new beginnings will come in the next month. Allow things to come to a close naturally, without resistance, blame, or criticism. Any unsettled feelings will resolve themselves next month. Focus on your accomplishments rather than on the past.

AUGUST (1 Personal Month): Renewed Energy, Cooperative Ventures

Joint projects or cooperative ventures take on new energy and direction. You are feeling reborn and ready to take on the world. Keep in mind that you are still in the early stages of your new epicycle; time is required to allow your ideas and projects to develop and reach maturity. Although you may be eager to move forward with your plans, remember that this is a 2 Personal Year, and as such, it requires that you wait while conditions mature and are made ready. Impatience will only set you back and cause feelings of frustration. Keep in mind that you will need the support of others to develop your projects, so keep those lines of communication open. Avoid being overly self-centered. An opportunity may arise where you can use your leadership skills to inspire others. Give of yourself generously.

SEPTEMBER (11/2 Personal Month): Intuition, Sensitivity, Idealism

This could be an intense month, with increased opportunities for interacting with others. You may experience some self-doubt now, especially if you have shared your plans with people who are not supportive of your ideas. You are particularly sensitive to the opinions of others. Stay away from negative people. With the heightened sensitivity of the Master number 11, you could feel inspired from deep within. Your intuition is highly tuned, and you may be guided by your inner voice, or through dreams to help others in some special way. Keep your feet on the ground and stay focused on your goals. Avoid reaching for more than you can handle. Above all, be tactful and diplomatic this month.

OCTOBER (3 Personal Month): Pleasure, Creativity, Relaxation

Following the intensity of last month, you are probably ready for a little fun time out now. Plan a vacation or some enjoyable outings with friends. Continue to be patient and to pace your efforts. Progress will come in due time. You are more playful, positive, and optimistic now, and your creativity is heightened. Try to express this creative energy in your work, or in your relationships. Take some time out for the arts, go to a movie, a standup comedy show, the theatre, or dust off your guitar and pick and make some music of your own. You could enjoy a romantic tête-à-tête. Avoid overly stressful situations this month.

NOVEMBER (13/4 Personal Month): Hard Work, Focus, Practicality

Hopefully you managed to take some fun time off last month, because now you'll need to get organized and focus on the tasks at hand. You could be feeling unfairly pressed to take care of details, or limited by the amount of work that is piling up on your desk. The most effective approach will be to simply get down to business. The more you resist and fight it, the more restricted you will feel. Before complaining about your burdens, keep in mind that this is a stabilizing month, and dealing with commitments and foundation issues will give you the strength and security to move forward with your plans next year. Put your nose to the grindstone and you will see results.

DECEMBER (5 Personal Month): Change, Surprises, Freedom

As much as last month forced you to deal with the details of your work, this month brings change and surprises. Be flexible. This is a good month for promoting yourself or your business. Use new and unusual approaches. Don't walk the beaten path; be innovative. Flexibility and open-mindedness will be an asset. You do need a bit of freedom and fun, so try to unload some of your excess responsibilities. Review your list of priorities and deal with the really important matters first. Save the menial tasks for later. Travel and new experiences are possible this month. It could be difficult for you to focus on responsibilities at this time.

The 2 Personal Year Workshop

Complete this workshop at the beginning of the year along with your yearly planning and goal setting.

1. Relative to your Life Path and Birth Day numbers and your personal experience of the number 2, how are you faring in your relationships, both personal and professional? Do you have difficulty relating to others or being attentive to the needs of those who are close to you? How do you feel about being receptive in general? Are you a go-getter, always in charge? If so, how do you get feedback from your environment if you are not receptive?

2. Go back to the last time you experienced a 2 Personal Year. (See the "My Personal History" exercise in chapter 3.) What was going on in your relationships at that time? How did you deal with your emotional responses to the circumstances of your life? Did you experience peace and harmony in your personal relationships? If not, why not? How did you react to new projects begun the previous year? Were you successful in overcoming any Phase II objections?

3. Relative to where you are in your life at this time, how would you like to see your relationships improve? For example, if you are a freedom-loving 5 Life Path person with a trail of broken relationships behind you, what might you do to bring stability into your relationships? If you are a deep-thinking 7 Life Path, consider how your solitary nature and specialness have affected your ability to build strong personal relationships. If you are a strong 8 type, usually caught up in career matters, how can you bring more balance into your life?

4. Review your Key Life Sectors list. Are all these sectors relevant in your life at this time? Have you set aside time for special relationships? If not, make any necessary changes or adjustments.

5. Take the time to heal relationship issues. Work on developing new business and professional relationships. Deepen old business and professional relationships. Get

in touch with clients/customers. Learn more about their needs. Take special time out for family. Update your relationships with your children. Their needs grow as they do. Give a little extra time to aging parents. They won't be around forever. Don't ignore those pesky customers. They may have something of value to convey to you. Pay attention to difficult relationships. They will teach you much about yourself.

6. Do you have any negative, Phase II types of responses or objections to your fresh new start of last year? If your objections stem from a negative attitude, such as fear of failure, self-criticism, excessive perfectionism, or lack of self-confidence, what can you do to change these destructive habits? Affirmations and creative visualization are examples of very effective tools for dealing with these types of behavior.

7. Would it be beneficial for you to develop a relationship with a mentor or coach? This would be a good time to join a peer advisory group. If there isn't one in your area, start one.

8. If you are taking a personal relationship to the next level, such as marriage, have you openly discussed your hopes, plans, and expectations for the future? Get things out in the open before you embark on a lifelong journey together. Explore your true motives for making this decision at this time. In this enlightened age, surprisingly, still too many people marry for the wrong reasons.

Exercise: Year-End Review

Complete this exercise at the end of your 2 Personal Year.

1. In what ways did you improve your relationships this year? What have you learned about being receptive and open to outside help?

2. What are the benefits of these changes?

3. What is the most important lesson you learned this year?

4. What new knowledge will you bring into your upcoming 3 Personal Year?

The 2 Personal Year Goal Setting and Planning Worksheet

As an aid to your yearly planning, complete the following worksheet. Set goals for each of your Key Life Sectors. In a 2 Personal Year, you should focus on relationships. Think before making decisions. Consider the impact of your actions on the people in your life. Your goals should reflect your values and desires at this time of your life.

Goal Setting and Planning Worksheet My 2 Personal Year Cooperation, Receptivity, Adaptability	
Key Life Sectors	*Goals for the year*
1	i
	ii
	iii
2	i
	ii
	iii
3	i
	ii
	iii
4	i
	ii
	iii
5	i
	ii
	iii
6	i
	ii
	iii

SIX

✦ ✦ ✦

Creativity, Self-Expression, Joie de Vivre

THE 3 PERSONAL YEAR

✳

1	2	3	4	5	6	7	8	9

When you move into a 3 Personal Year, it is not unusual to experience a feeling of relief, like a valve opening up, releasing built-up steam. The joining of one with another, the 2 experienced last year, now produces a third energy, just as the fusion of sperm and egg produces an embryo. The energy of the 3 Personal Year helps relieve much of the tension caused by the polarization of forces that was experienced in the previous 2 Personal Year. Last year the focus was on balancing all aspects of relationships. It was self versus other; seeing that my needs are met while yours are being met.

In the 3 Year, energy explodes, possibilities abound, and what seemed previously guarded and tentative, too sensitive to be brought forth, too vulnerable to be exposed to external scrutiny and potential criticism, now begins to bubble to the surface. New projects and ideas that emerged over the past two years are now seeking an outlet for uninhibited manifestation. What was on your mind is ready to be expressed.

During the 3 Personal Year, you will find the pace of activity stepping up considerably. Last year, in your 2 Personal Year, you may have encountered delays, objections, or reactions—some internal, some external, some expected, others not—to your previous 1 Personal Year initiatives. You may have felt that things were not moving as quickly as you would have liked. Forget the past, that trend will change this year. The expanding energy of the number 3 will offer you multiple opportunities to be social, have more fun, and express yourself in whatever medium you enjoy, whether through writing, painting, speaking, theatre, crafts, socializing, or good old-fashioned dinner parties. You will generally have more personal freedom to do all those things that you are eager to accomplish.

Doors open more easily in a 3 Personal Year. People make things happen for you, and income can increase. This is an excellent year to broaden your relationship spheres and to expand your personal and business network of contacts. You express yourself well now, and can get your ideas across with creative flair and originality.

Michel, a 22/4 Life Path with an 11/2 Birth Day, is a highly gifted musician and composer. In a 3 Personal Year, he was invited to participate with two other composers in the production and recording of their cello sonatas for a promotional CD. This welcome opportunity was also accompanied by a public concert. All this came about through knowing the right people in the right places. It isn't uncommon for people to catch lucky breaks under a 3 influence. Interestingly, Michel's cello sonata had initially been composed in the 1 Personal Year of the previous epicycle. Often, projects begun in a 1 Personal Year are not brought to completion right away; by the same token, it does not necessarily follow that everything you begin in a 1 Year will become a great accomplishment.

This book was produced in a burst of creative energy during a 3 Personal Year, a record for me, since it had previously taken me twenty years to complete two other works. Additionally, in that same year, I set up the structure for three other writing projects. If you have a creative side, you may find that the 3 Year can be a very fertile period.

The 3 Personal Year has the potential for being a really fun year, as it favors shared pleasures, personal expression, social expansion, creativity, affection, relationships, love, romance, personal freedom, and finances. To avoid waste and dispersion of your energies, you will have to work at keeping things focused. Moderation is key now. Avoid hasty decision making; remember to think things through and to apply restraint. In a 3 Personal Year there can be a tendency of being extravagant, perhaps even overly optimistic, especially if you have many 3s among your core numbers.

With opportunities on the rise, it's easy to become scattered. You could find yourself taking on far too many projects. In the end, you'll be disappointed since you'll have to abandon the extra activities, even though they seemed like good ideas at the time. Just because something looks good doesn't mean that you are obligated to take it on. It's important to keep an eye on your long-term goals now. But focusing on your goals doesn't have to feel like a chore or a restricting obligation. Use your creativity to stay on track.

An excellent and fun tool for helping you stay focused is to make a collage that depicts your goals. Cut out pictures from magazines. Pin them to your wall or on a bulletin board next to your work area. I keep a binder with a section for each of my Key Life Sectors. For each Sector, I have specific goals that are represented by pictures. For example, in the writing section, I have a picture of a book cover for each of my book projects. In my home projects section, I paste photos for the renovations I want to complete in my house. As goals are reached, I remove the pages; I add new ones when they are needed. It may sound a little grade-schoolish, but, besides being lots of fun, having clear pictures can help you stay on track. What's more, who ever said that planning and goal setting couldn't be fun?

For some people, creativity is a tender commodity, to be treated delicately and with great nurturing. In a world that generally favors conventions over originality, it can be difficult to break through the confines of conformity and dare to express ideas that go against the common currents. You may have to handle your creative ideas with care. Avoid discussing your fledgling ideas with people who may not be in line with your thinking. For some reason, it seems that it is easier for many people to find fault in something new than it is to see its qualities or potential value. If your best friend is habitually negative and critical, don't discuss your new idea with him. Instead, find someone you trust, someone who has a positive attitude, and someone who will be supportive rather than destructive. Most people have enough self-destructive ammunition within themselves as it is. You certainly don't need to leave home to find more!

If you wish to prevent the destruction of your dreams and give them a fighting chance against Phase II Thinking, consciously channel energy into your creative-thinking process this year. If you haven't dealt with your Phase II Thinking, you might find yourself being overly critical of any fresh, new ideas. Decide now to have a positive attitude toward yourself and your projects.

If you habitually maintain negative thinking habits, now would be an excellent time for an attitude adjustment. Practice saying *yes* instead of *no*. In a 3 Personal Year, typically you will have plenty of opportunities to practice saying yes, as you are more socially inclined and more optimistic than usual. In a 3 Year, people are inclined to approach you more readily for a variety of requests and opportunities. Don't worry, once you've reached your quota and your calendar is full, you can learn to politely say no. Simply explain that you are fully booked but would love to help out next time. In a recent 3 Personal Year, hardly a week went by where I didn't get an invitation to participate in some sort of fundraising, social, or business event.

Epp, a financial security advisor, came up with what she felt was a fabulous idea to promote her business. She visualized herself hosting a wine-and-cheese and art-appreciation fundraiser in a gallery for her clients and friends. She saw this as a way of promoting the friendlier side of herself while deepening relationships with the people who could drive business her way, an excellent business approach for a highly competitive field. We had already discussed the creative possibilities available to her, given that she was now in a 3 Personal Year. She sounded very excited as she described her plan to me over the phone, but as she approached the end of her story, I could hear the "yeah buts" pushing to the surface, ready to cast dark shadows on her bright new idea. And then the Phase II Thinking kicked in.

When we took a closer look at her perceived objections, she quickly came to realize that they were symbolic of her old way of negative thinking. In fact, she soon discovered there was no real foundation for her objections. At this point, she reaffirmed her intention to adjust her attitude and proceeded to work on the action plan that would ensure the success of her new marketing venture. As it turned out, the event was a great success, and raised far more money than she had initially anticipated.

Over the course of many years, Linda, a 3 Life Path with a 3 Birth Day, explored a variety of career options, including aesthetics, therapeutic massage, modeling, and style and image consulting. Her positive attitude and friendly disposition allowed her to pursue each of these avenues with a certain degree of success, though she feels that she was very scattered throughout most of her life. Until her mid-forties, she had not quite fully tapped into her truly creative and artistic side. In a 3 Personal Year and having also progressed into a 3 Life Path Period (See "The Life Path Periods," chapter 13), Linda's creativity found a perfect outlet. Now in a happy and loving relationship, she was able to return to one of her early passions, the world of watercolor. She took lessons and started to experiment with a variety of materials, until in a matter of a few years, she became fully engaged as a painter. Her works are now being sold in a variety of galleries and on the Internet.

There are many ways of expressing creativity. Not everyone is a potential Picasso, Shakespeare, or Mozart. In your 3 Personal Year, look for ways of being creative in each of your Key Life Sectors. By the same token, just because you enjoy music, painting, or writing, it doesn't necessarily follow that in your next 3 Personal Year you will be discovered as the next Beethoven, Degas, or Tom Clancy. Your luck will come through if you have paid your dues. Of course, that's stating the obvious, you say. But you'd be surprised at the number of people who believe they will one day suddenly, somehow be discovered, without ever having to develop their talents or skills.

Unleashing Your Creative Power

Over the years, I've often heard the words "One day, I'm going to write a book" or "One day I'll learn to play the guitar, or take singing lessons, or learn to paint. . . ." The list is endless. I don't know about you, but my calendar still says Monday, Tuesday, Wednesday, Thursday, Friday, Saturday, and Sunday, and . . . guess what? No "one day." The closest you'll ever get to that elusive "one day" is probably the 3 Personal Year. This is when you are most likely to feel free to express yourself.

Unless applied directly to your business, artistic and creative activities usually do not generate income, at least not in the short term, so mostly they will be relegated to the pile of not-so-important things to do. Even if you have no plans for selling your artwork, or publishing, or performing, or selling your refinished old desk, or patenting your invention, creative self-expression is in and of itself a richly rewarding experience. If you should decide to incorporate a creative outlet into your life, an effective way to do this is to set aside specific time slots in your agenda for this activity. Begin by determining a schedule that is appropriate for your craft. Make this time sacrosanct. Many writers do their best work early in the morning. Painters may prefer early afternoons, for lighting, and budding musicians might enjoy strumming their guitars in the quiet late-night hours. Find a time that works for you.

Create an environment that is conducive to your craft, and free of noise, clutter, and distractions. Feed the kids and the cat, walk the dog, return your mother's call, pay that late bill—before you enter your sacred creating space. Make yourself a pot of coffee or tea and turn off the phone. Make certain your workspace is ergonomic. Don't read your e-mail, don't even download it during your practice or working time. Hang a sign on your door that says *Genius at Work: Do Not Disturb*. Depending on your craft, you may want to set a mood with music. Don't be hesitant to let people know that this activity is important to you.

Once you begin the process of creating, your creative juices will naturally be unleashed. This creative energy will infuse all of your thought processes and you might even see creative possibilities all around you. You may need to rein yourself in at times, as your creativity starts to wander and you lose focus. Once unleashed, you may find that you get your most brilliant ideas at the most inopportune times. Don't risk losing a morsel of your brilliance. Keep a notebook, sketchbook, laptop, or recorder handy. A tiny germ of an idea could eventually grow into a significant line of thought, and tiny germs are so easily lost. Above all, relax and enjoy the process. It doesn't really matter whether or not your work is published, performed, or sold. Your creativity alone will take you on an incredible journey of self-discovery. You will uncover aspects of yourself that would otherwise never have seen the light of day. Your creative process will in effect transform you.

The 3 Personal Year Month by Month

Note that the following descriptions for the Personal Months are to be used as guidelines for determining possible scenarios. Use the keywords from chapter 1 to interpret potential trends that apply to your particular lifestyle. Each person is unique, and each has a unique relationship with the numbers. Also keep in mind that the Personal Month trends are secondary to the Personal Year trends, and should be considered along with your Life Path and Birth Date numbers as well as your current Personal Year number.

JANUARY (4 Personal Month): *Work, Progress, Organization*

Don't plan a vacation this month. This creative year begins with a month of hard work. Your drive and focus combined with a positive attitude inspire others to follow suit. If you want to ensure that this year is as productive as possible, establish a detailed action plan for important projects and goals. Get yourself organized and eliminate time wasters from your life. A 3 Personal Year can be fun and exciting, but at the same time quite distracting. If you have a solid plan in place, you can always use it to nudge yourself back in line if you do become sidetracked. Be practical, attend to details, make sensible dietary choices, and schedule regular exercise. Establish a healthy daily routine early in the year, before things become too hectic. Your creativity will have a solid foundation on which to build.

FEBRUARY (5 Personal Month): Expansion, Change, Freedom

This month can prove to be a bit chaotic, as surprises and unexpected events arise, forcing you to be flexible in your planning. Be aware of a tendency to become sidetracked. Keep your long-term goals in mind; refer to your action plan, while allowing yourself the chance to explore new possibilities as they arise. This is a social time, with new opportunities for growth and expansion. However, avoid impulsive or irresponsible choices or behavior. There may be a tendency for excesses of food, alcohol, or other sensual pleasures. Enjoy your free time, travel, take a vacation, and have some fun. Don't take on more responsibilities than you can handle this month. Be resourceful.

MARCH (6 Personal Month): Responsibility, Service, Healing

You certainly won't be alone much this month! People call on you for a variety of reasons, and if you work in a service-related field, you will be busier than ever. You have lots of great ideas and can communicate them easily. Others enjoy your company, as they appreciate your creative approach to problem-solving. Quality time spent with family and friends will go a long way toward healing old wounds. Enjoy the love and affection of your significant other. Maintain a giving, non-judgmental, and compassionate attitude. In your efforts to be helpful, be aware of a tendency to be overly helpful; others might perceive you as meddlesome or interfering. Maintain balance in all sectors of activity.

APRIL (7 Personal Month): Reflection, Analysis, Solitude

The energy of the number 7 requires that you take some time out for meditation and inner reflection or simply enjoying quiet activities such as reading, gardening, or going for long walks in the park. Since this is a 3 Personal Year, a year of creative self-expression and heightened mental activity, this is a good time to explore an artistic outlet such as journaling, drawing, or painting as it can help release those inner messages and inspirations. Reflect on how you can best use your creativity throughout the rest of this year. You could be feeling less inclined to go out and socialize, seeking a pause from your busy social calendar, but you experience an endless flow of creative ideas. Despite your need for solitude, remain in touch with those who are close.

MAY (8 Personal Month): Accomplishment, Power, Action

Using creative approaches, you can make excellent progress in business and career this month. You have earned the respect of your superiors and now is the time to collect. The relationships you built in your previous 2 Personal Year are starting to pay off. Combine enthusiasm, optimism, and self-confidence to create business opportunities. This is a power month, time to push forward with your plans, take advantage of opportunities. Be bold and daring in the pursuit of practical and realistic goals. You deal effectively with money and finances. You may feel as though luck is on your side. Your positive attitude opens doors and invites the support of others.

JUNE (9 Personal Month): Completion, Endings, Release

It's time to finish off projects and bring closure where required. Review your goals for the year. Are you on track, or did you get sidetracked? If you have set short- to medium-term goals, measure your progress and make adjustments as necessary. It often happens in a 3 Personal Year that we become distracted and get involved in projects that are not quite in keeping with our long-term goals. Take a close look at how you are spending your time and resources. Do a little housecleaning. Get rid of what isn't working or what isn't important. It's not unusual to feel a little lost or emotional in a 9 Personal Month. Be compassionate and understanding. Spend some time helping others, taking the focus off you. Be patient. Get some rest. A new cycle begins next month.

JULY (1 Personal Month): Self-Expression, Energy, Enthusiasm

The blues you may have been feeling last month are gone now and you feel reinvigorated, energetic, and enthusiastic again. You can find new ways of expressing yourself, and if you have creative or artistic projects on the go, you will feel inspired to produce new work. Take advantage of the opportunities presented through your social network. This is the time to go for it. Explore and express your uniqueness. You may feel ready to make important changes, to break out of your routine, or even move away from an unrewarding job or start your own business. If you have not yet explored your creativity, you may have the urge to journal or write. Your social calendar fills up again and you are drawn to new activities.

AUGUST (11/2 Personal Month): Receptivity, Inspiration, Patience

You may be feeling a little Phase II effect, following your burst of energy and enthusiasm of last month. Keep in mind that self-doubt is common, especially if you have made some important changes in your personal or professional life in the past year. Be patient and wait for projects to develop in their own time. You are particularly sensitive this month, and should protect yourself from any negative influences. Avoid discussing your new plans with those who could criticize and talk you out of them. You feel inspired, but at the same time anxious, nervous, and fragile. Nurture your inspiration. You could come up with unique solutions for the problems of someone in your environment.

SEPTEMBER (3 Personal Month): Creativity, Joie de Vivre

Your calendar fills up with all sorts of social events this month, and if you've been working on a creative project, you're probably bursting at the seams with inspiration. Self-expression comes easily, whether in your work, relationships, or creative projects. Your enthusiasm is at an all-time high, and you inspire others with your optimism and cheery good nature. Focus on the more creative aspects of your work; try new approaches, express yourself freely and joyfully. If you are still uncertain about your projects, be careful not to fall in the trap of excessive analysis and criticism. Keep a positive attitude. Make new contacts, explore new networking opportunities, renew or nurture existing friendships. Take time out for enjoyment. Have a dinner party; celebrate the abundance of the autumn harvest.

OCTOBER (4 Personal Month): Organization, Discipline, Focus

With the 4 Personal Year rapidly approaching, you could be starting to feel the pressure of work and heavy obligations weighing you down. Contrary to this year, which brought out opportunities for self-expression, joy, and socialization, next year will require much more focus and attention to detail. Use your creative ideas to organize yourself so that you don't have to fuss over details. Arrangee your workspace so that it is efficient and also pleasant to be in, especially if you foresee spending many hours there. Take care of your health. Maintain that enthusiasm and positive attitude as you get down to business. Find joy in being disciplined, knowing that the hard work will pay off with tangible results in the next year.

NOVEMBER (14/5 Personal Month): The Unexpected, Change, Travel

Use a pencil to mark entries into your calendar this month; you'll probably need to make frequent changes as unexpected circumstances arise. This can be an exciting few weeks, with opportunities for socializing, adventure, and travel. Resist the urge to quit or make impulsive decisions. Just because things don't seem to be moving as quickly as you would like them to doesn't mean they aren't going at the pace they are meant to be going. Be patient. Don't make radical moves unless you are absolutely certain they are right for you. Stick to some level of routine, and avoid erratic behavior. Take the time to learn from your errors. To keep focused on your goals and tasks, offer yourself a reward for each level of completion. Keep some free time in your schedule so as not to feel overly trapped with obligations.

DECEMBER (6 Personal Month): Love, Relationships, Harmony

You are likely to enjoy a wonderful, fun-filled holiday season with family and friends this year. The creative inspiration and joie de vivre of this 3 Personal Year will extend to lavish dinner parties and social gatherings. A close friend or family member may need your support. Your sense of responsibility runs high, and feelings of love and caring are strong. You may be ready to commit to a long-term relationship. This is a rewarding time all around, especially for business, finances, and career. This has been a busy year, with some very hectic moments, and you may be feeling the need for a little peace and quiet. Although quiet times will be at a premium, choose calm and harmonious environments and activities over noisy and chaotic ones. A little balance and peacefulness will help soothe your soul. Most likely, as you tend to family business, this will be a fine ending to a busy and fun year.

The 3 Personal Year Workshop

Complete this workshop at the beginning of the year along with your yearly planning and goal setting.

1. Relative to your Life Path, Birth Day number, and personal experience of the number 3, do you feel that you have sufficient avenues for expressing your creativity? Keep in mind that you don't have to be a Picasso to be creative. Each of us has a creative genius deep inside. Are you expressing your ideas freely in your work? At home? In your leisure activities?

2. Go back to the last time you experienced a 3 Personal Year. (See the "My Personal History" exercise in chapter 3.) What was going on in your life at that time? Were you able to let go and have fun? Did you experience romance? Were you able to develop a positive attitude toward life? How did you express your creativity? Did you have a tendency to be distracted or disorganized?

3. Relative to where you are in your life at this time, how would you like to see your life improved and made more fun? For example, if you are a workaholic 4 or 8 Life Path, have you forgotten how to laugh and enjoy life? When was the last time you took your spouse on a date? Your family on a vacation? Went out for a show? Which areas of your life require more of your creative input? Is there any romance in your life?

4. Review your Key Life Sectors list. Are all these sectors still relevant in your life at this time? Are fun and play included among your Key Life Sectors? Is creativity? Entertainment? Romance? If not, make any necessary changes or adjustments.

5. Identify a sector in your life where you feel you would like to express yourself more freely, more creatively. This can be for business, home, family, or pleasure. If you have never expressed your creativity, try taking up journal writing, sketching, or even singing in the car. You'd be surprised at how liberating it can be to free your voice and sing along with the radio or CD player.

6. Work on improving your communication skills. In all areas, focus on expressing your true thoughts and desires. Network, socialize, and meet people. Don't stay shut up in your home. Go out; enjoy the company of friends and family. Go out on a limb and have a dinner party. Join Toastmasters or volunteer for social events at your local church or community center.

7. Relax and above all, learn to laugh. If you need an attitude adjustment, focus on the positive. Watch comedies; read funny books or comics. Read books on the power of positive thinking. Find ways of bringing joy into your daily life. This may seem silly, but there are so many people who have forgotten the art of simply enjoying life.

Exercise: Year-End Review

Complete this exercise at the end of your 3 Personal Year.

1. In what ways did you bring more joy into your life this year? Did you manifest your creativity? Did you free up your self-expression? In what ways did you expand your social spheres?

2. What are the benefits of these changes?

3. What is the most important lesson you learned this year?

4. What new knowledge will you bring into your upcoming 4 Personal Year?

The 3 Personal Year Goal Setting and Planning Worksheet

As an aid to your yearly planning, complete the following worksheet. Set goals for each of your Key Life Sectors. In a 3 Personal Year, you should be focusing on creative self-expression, your social life, and the joy of living. This year could bring much luck. Your goals should reflect your values and desires at this time of your life.

Goal Setting and Planning Worksheet My 3 Personal Year Creativity, Self-Expression, Joie de Vivre	
Key Life Sectors	*Goals for the year*
1	i
	ii
	iii
2	i
	ii
	iii
3	i
	ii
	iii
4	i
	ii
	iii
5	i
	ii
	iii
6	i
	ii
	iii

SEVEN

Dedication, Focus, Organization

THE 4 PERSONAL YEAR

There are three keywords that accurately describe the tone of the 4 Personal Year: work, work, and more work! Whether you like it or not, you will find that this year your energies will be best spent attending to the details and responsibilities of home, family, and work. This is not a time for grand ideas, making a big splash, or fast and furious growth and expansion. Essentially, you will need to focus on the meat-and-potatoes matters.

Last year, a 3 Personal Year brought some exciting new ideas, perhaps a little shaking-up of your social life, some romance, a little fun, and probably a variety of experiences. Moving into the 4 energy is a bit like adding a fourth leg to a three-legged chair. It has a stabilizing effect. However, this stabilization means that you won't be able to wander off and give in to distractions, at least for a while. If you allowed yourself to be scattered and veered off course last year, now you will have the opportunity to get back on track.

You have just begun the second phase of your 9-Year Epicycle, the productive phase. You could be feeling a sense of urgency, a growing desire to accomplish something tangible, to make things happen. Last year, your mind was filled with ideas. You may have shared some of these great ideas with friends. It's time now to pass from ideas to action.

This year your projects take form and become real. Whatever you set in motion at the start of this epicycle should be showing signs of life. If you started a new business, you will need to concentrate on bookkeeping, organization, and generating income. You will know where your business stands, and if your foundation is solid, you should begin to see some substantial results. Even if you're not beating out the competition yet, you are becoming a serious contender. This year should move you forward significantly.

On the other hand, if your new ideas of the past couple of years lacked substance, then they are not likely to survive. You could find yourself going back to the drawing board, looking for a new way to earn a living. If this is the case, you may find that your options are limited. You will have to work very hard to find something satisfactory.

The 4 Personal Year can be a very productive year if you dedicate yourself, focus, and commit to your obligations. Concentrate on the details and the groundwork. Revise your budget, track your spending and earnings, and invest wisely. This can be a good year for making money. Sustained effort, perseverance, and discipline will help you not only overcome obstacles, but also build a solid foundation for your future accomplishments. The work you do now may lack glamour and may even seem to be going nowhere, but it is certain to contribute to your achievement in the 8 Personal Year, the peak of the cycle. Keep in mind that the years flow organically from one to the other, each year contributing toward the fulfillment of your goals. During the 4 Year in particular, you can make significant progress.

This will be a difficult year if you refuse to buckle down and focus on the work at hand. If you are not accustomed to discipline and hard work, you could become resentful about the restrictions and limitations you encounter when dealing with your responsibilities and duties. The 4 is the most grounded number and requires a realistic approach. It's not time for fantasy and pie-in-the-sky daydreaming. Things will go much more smoothly if you get real with yourself.

If you feel overwhelmed with details and obligations, revise your plan. Trim back the fat. Make a smaller garden. Make fewer promises. Walk, don't run. There is no law that says you have to do it all, at least not all in one year. Many people have difficulty lowering their expectations, downsizing, and slowing down. A 4 Personal Year requires a lean and mean management style. Focus on essentials. Delegate or simply abandon what is superfluous. Fatigue and stress-related health issues can surface in a 4 Year. Be reasonable in all areas and, in particular, ensure a proper diet and get some exercise.

In a 4 Personal Year, home and family obligations can become a priority. A typical 4 Year often involves time and money spent renovating or decorating a home. Young adults leave home and rooms are reassigned. You may want to reorganize your workspace, make it more ergonomic or more efficient. This is a great time to hire a personal organizer and to clear your work and living spaces of clutter. A good system will make your work easier and more fun.

It's not uncommon to tend to the needs of an aging parent or ailing family member in a 4 Year. At the age of 73, Denise found herself caring full-time for her husband of fifty years. He had developed a severe case of shingles following a series of chemotherapy treatments for a rare blood cancer and required round-the-clock care. Denise could barely leave the house long enough to buy groceries. Although she attended to her husband's needs without a word of complaint, at the end of that 4 Year, she was clearly exhausted.

Organize your personal and business matters now so you can effectively make plans for the expansion and renewed activity you will experience next year, a 5 Personal Year. Refusing to accept responsibility at this time can lead to poor preparation and eventually to missed opportunities. Avoid wallowing in self-pity and complaints. Face your responsibilities head on, and deal with the issues that are in front of you. After all, you put yourself in your current position.

By dealing with issues directly, you will feel empowered. Consolidate your activities. This is not a time for wastefulness. Use your resources wisely. Make the best of what you have. You should have all the tools you need at your disposal at this time to set yourself up for future success. Settle down, put down some roots, put your nose to the grindstone, and take care of business. Here is an opportunity to get the job done and actually enjoy the work. This can be a very productive year.

If you have a 4 among your core numbers, a 4 Life Path, for example, you may be quite comfortable with this focused energy, because it feels familiar and safe. At the same time, you might want to guard against being overly rigid and driving yourself into a rut. Routine may feel safe and comfortable, but in the long term it can prevent you from taking on new challenges and limit your growth potential. A healthy balance of focus and flexibility will help you derive more from your opportunities this year.

My clients often miss their annual appointments in their 4 Personal Years, unless their birthdays fall at the end of the year, at which point they generally come with their tongue hanging down to their chins, exhausted and often discouraged from the seemingly endless amount of work that has somehow piled up in their lives. They all agree that the 4 Year is one of hard work!

Yet at the same time, it's possible to lose focus and become overly caught up with the job and money in a 4 Personal Year. Niki, a 3 Life Path with a 3 Birth Day had taken up singing early in her previous epicycle. She had cut a CD and experienced a few club gigs, but her career as a jazz singer didn't generate enough income to justify quitting her day job. In her 4 Personal Year, she focused all her time and energy on her demanding management job, leaving her no time for music. Toward the end of the year, she realized that she had reached a plateau. Although it paid well, her job did not give her the satisfaction that singing in front of an audience gave her. She decided to look for a less demanding job, one that would allow her the opportunity to spend more time on her true passion.

Celebrate Adversity . . . It May Be the Key to Your Success!

Your greatest enemy may very well be the one thing you long for the most in life: ease. Ah yes . . . the easy life, the good life, a life of peace and quiet. Wouldn't it be nice to never have to struggle, to never have to deal with problems on a daily basis, to never have to fight for what you want? Sounds like a nice thought? But is a life of ease and comfort an asset or a liability? If you were not required to work for a living, would you? If you didn't have to overcome personal and professional challenges, would you still work your way up the competitive career ladder? If you didn't have to push yourself, would you develop your abilities? If an athlete didn't train, would he qualify for the Olympics?

From what I've seen over the years, in hundreds of consultations, most people don't move much unless they are faced with some form of challenge, either from pain, dissatisfaction, or adversity. For some reason or other, we seem to be hard-wired that way. Sometimes, it takes a really difficult period, one during which all the important aspects of life seem to be in crisis at the same time: divorce, the loss of a job, dealing with a troubled teen, an illness. Only then do we cry out, "Stop! There's got to be a better way," and only then will we get up and do something about it.

Surprisingly, during the easy periods we are less likely to reach within our depths and pull out our talents and abilities and express the best of ourselves. Sad, but true. When things are easy, we slack off. When times are tough, we express a wide range of responses, which can include indignation, anger, discouragement, fear, sadness, panic, anxiety, and the ever-popular self-pity. Never have I heard a client exclaim, after being made aware of an upcoming difficult transition, "Hurray! Here comes a great opportunity for me to push myself beyond my comfort zone, to learn about myself and to grow, to hone my skills and become a better person! I think I will go out and celebrate my 4 Personal Year of hard work!"

How many times has an opportunity for growth, learning, and self-betterment crossed your path? Probably a lot more times than you realize. Tragedies such as the death of a loved one, illness, or the loss of employment all provide you with such opportunities, but so do the simple circumstances of your day-to-day life, such as an encounter with an angry client, a misunderstanding with your spouse or child, or a traffic jam that makes you late for an important meeting. Whether big or small, each challenge provides an opportunity for learning and growth. A typical 4 Personal Year provides an abundance of challenges, some big, some small, but all requiring your dedication, focus, and attention.

The important thing to remember is that life comes from within, not from without. It isn't determined by the boulders you encounter along the way, but rather by the way you think of and then deal with these obstacles. Your life is a result of the choices you make, and these choices are based on several things, including an understanding of yourself, an understanding of the nature of life and its cycles, your willingness to tap into your resources, both inner and outer, and your readiness to accept full responsibility for your decisions.

The next time you are faced with adversity, whether major or minor, you might stop and ask yourself, *What can I learn from this situation? How can I grow? How can I become a better person? How can I be more productive, a better contributor to the world around me? What can I do to help the situation at hand?* Don't shrink from adversity and lie in waiting for easy street. You'll stagnate. And the next time a very big boulder falls on your path, gather up your friends and go out and celebrate; the most challenging times are the ones that will provide you with the greatest opportunities for growth!

The 4 Personal Year Month by Month

Note that the following descriptions for the Personal Months are to be used as guidelines for determining possible scenarios. Use the keywords from chapter 1 to interpret potential trends that apply to your particular lifestyle. Each person is unique, and each has a unique relationship with the numbers. Also keep in mind that the Personal Month trends are secondary to the Personal Year trends, and should be considered along with your Life Path and Birth Date numbers as well as your current Personal Year number.

JANUARY (5 Personal Month): New Opportunities, Change

Your last year, a 3 Personal Year, may have brought you many opportunities to enjoy life, and you could be feeling the trend continuing this month. Take your time in deciding on any new endeavors, especially if you aren't 100 percent certain of your choice. Avoid hasty decisions. Things may not be as they appear on the surface. This is a year of focus and hard work, so pick your battles carefully. You will be stuck dealing with many details over the next several months. Be prepared to work hard. You may wonder if all this work is worth the effort. You could make an interesting new business contact this month. Do take some free time off this month, perhaps a weekend getaway. The break will recharge your batteries and prepare you for the work ahead.

FEBRUARY (6 Personal Month): Nurturing, Balance, Creativity

If you take the time to organize your home and family life this month, things will run more smoothly throughout the year. Set up a calendar to schedule chores; share responsibilities with all members of the household. This will leave you with more time to spend together. A little affection and TLC will go a long way in providing you with the support and encouragement you need now. Your efforts at work are recognized and you may take on additional responsibilities. People come to you for advice and support. Maintain balance and harmony in your life; this is a time of healing. Take on a fun project with your partner or children. Redecorate the family room; install a home theatre system. Relationships are stable now.

MARCH (7 Personal Month): Pause, Reflection, Solitude

This is a good time to pause and reflect on your goals. Are you on track, or have you been distracted over the past few months? Take the time for research and study. Rest and focus on your health. Revise your plan. Are your goals realistic? Keep in mind that this is a 4 Personal Year, and you should be tending to the essentials. Are you managing your time well? You are able to solve complex problems with innovative solutions. Delegate some of the more menial tasks and spend some time in quiet thought. You are not feeling particularly sociable this month; don't let friends talk you into parties and late nights out if you'd rather be alone. You seek the meaning of life as your mind travels deeper into your inner self. You could receive important insights from within. Meditate.

APRIL (8 Personal Month): Power, Results, Advancement

If you have paid attention to details and focused on the work at hand, this month should be very rewarding, both personally and financially. This is when dedication and hard work pay off. You feel on top of your game now, and the results are showing that your efforts have been worth it. More than ever, you are focused and determined to reach your goals. This is an excellent month for advancement on all levels, especially professionally and financially. Go for the money. Being in a 4 Year, remember to keep both feet on the ground and remain practical. There is much work yet to be done this year. Proceed with confidence; this is a time of great material accomplishment. You are focused on career issues this month, and family is likely to take a back seat.

MAY (9 Personal Month): Completion, Endings, Release

You may find relief as a work project reaches completion this month. Having worked hard over the past few months, you may be feeling a bit tired and in need of a break. If you can't manage a vacation, try to take some time off, even if it is only a long weekend. Put your feet up; go for a long drive in the country. Take care of your health. Your emotions are running high, and you could find yourself overdramatizing situations, especially as you bring matters to a close. A work-related relationship could end. You would find reward in doing some community or volunteer work. Finish home projects, clean out the garage, remove clutter from your life. The more organized you are, the more productive you will be throughout the remainder of this year.

JUNE (1 Personal Month): Energy Renewal, Productivity

New work projects present themselves, or new career opportunities come to you now. Although you are inspired to move forward with your plans and perhaps even take on more work, keep in mind that progress will be slow in a 4 Personal Year and results may not be immediately visible. Your continued diligence and attention to detail will keep things moving forward. You will need to be patient this month. Keep some balance in your life, so as not to burn out. It's easy to forget about everything and throw yourself into your work, especially when you are feeling energized. To avoid getting stuck in a rut, try a new approach and break up the monotony of your daily routine. Take a different route to work; rearrange your workspace.

JULY (11/2 Personal Month): Relationships, Intuition, Cooperation

In order to accomplish your goals, you may need to work closely with others this month. Progress may seem slow, and you may not see eye-to-eye with colleagues. Your intuition is providing you with insights that may guide you to thinking and acting "outside the box." Your colleagues or partners may not be open to progressive solutions right now, and you could feel left out or ignored. This isn't the time to take things personally. Remember, keep your eye on the ball; be realistic. Save your unique ideas for later; they will eventually find a place. Patience and cooperation are key now as you work to strengthen the relationships you need to reach your goals. Use your encounters with others to deepen your knowledge of yourself. Find guidance and comfort from within.

AUGUST (3 Personal Month): Social Life, Creativity, Practicality

Work demands might lighten a bit this month, so try to take a break from work, without completely losing your momentum. A vacation would give you the renewal of optimism and energy that you will need to continue with your hard work in the months that follow. If you can't take a vacation, plan a dinner party with friends at home. Take time with family as well. Work on a creative or artistic project at home. Spend some time on your hobby, listening to music or going for leisurely drives in the country. Your mind is open to down-to-earth inspiration, helping you find practical solutions to everyday problems. Harness a positive outlook by acknowledging the progress achieved this year to date. Look for creative ways of making the work more fun.

SEPTEMBER (13/4 Personal Month): Limitation, Doubt, Work

This month could prove stressful as your workload rises substantially. You will need, more than ever, to focus on details and to keep your goals in mind. Draw on your feelings of optimism from last month to get you through. Maintain a healthy diet and exercise routine. Revise your budget; curb your spending. Although things appear to be moving far more slowly than you would like, it is necessary that you focus on foundation issues. Reorganize your plan if it lacks structure. Don't overlook the more tedious, basic aspects of your work. Remind yourself that hard work unfailingly leads to rewards. You get out of life what you put into it. Now is the time to see this principle at work. Tremendous opportunities are just around the corner; a solid foundation will ensure your success.

OCTOBER (5 Personal Month): Expansion, Adventure, Opportunity

You will be feeling relieved and much more free as the accumulated pressures of the previous months dissipate. If you worked hard last month, you will be ready to consider the new opportunities that are opening up before you. Remember to stay focused on your long-term goals, and to not jump on the first glossy opportunity that arises. This is an excellent time to promote yourself and your business. Your circle of contacts grows, and your new acquaintances could be very supportive of your endeavors. Be flexible and open-minded. Consider new ways of doing things. Creativity abounds. Break from the routine a bit, without losing track of your direction. The coming year will bring plenty of opportunity for growth and expansion.

NOVEMBER (6 Personal Month): Service, Responsibility, Family

Your attention is required on the home front. A family member may require your care, assistance, or support. Be kind, understanding, and sympathetic as you try to find practical solutions to the problems of others. Spend a little extra time at home, either working on a renovation project or in a relaxing activity with family and friends. Reestablish balance and harmony in your routine if you have been drawn off track by the exciting developments of last month. This is an excellent time for creative self-expression. If you are working on an art, drama, music, or writing project, your work could progress nicely. Revise your diet and get back to your workout routine. This can be a rewarding month as your superiors praise your work.

DECEMBER (7 Personal Month): Analysis, Study, Reflection

This challenging year of hard work and foundation is drawing to a close. You can reward yourself now by measuring your progress, based on the goals you set for yourself at the start of this epicycle, in your 1 Personal Year. You will need some quiet time by yourself to reflect and reevaluate your situation. Review your long-term goals. Doing so now will prevent you from being led astray in the coming months as you move into a 5 Personal

Year, a year of change, surprises, and unexpected occurrences. Spend some time walking in the woods; enjoy the peaceful quiet of nature. Reconnect with your inner spirit. Listen for new guidance and wisdom. Your inner peace and contentment will naturally flow outward to all your relationships. You are not much of a party animal this month.

The 4 Personal Year Workshop

Complete this workshop at the beginning of the year along with your yearly planning and goal setting.

1. Relative to your Life Path, Birth Day number, and personal experience of the number 4, are you prepared to focus and work hard toward the accomplishment of your goals? Are your work and home environments well organized? If you are a party-loving 3 Life Path, you may find it difficult to get focused now.

2. Go back to the last time you experienced a 4 Personal Year. What was going on in your life at that time? Did you feel limited or restricted by the obligations of your job or family? Were you well organized, or did you have trouble focusing on the work at hand? Did you experience illness?

3. Relative to where you are in your life at this time, how can you reorganize your life to make things easier, both at home and at work? Having an efficient routine and being well organized can make all the difference in making a 4 Personal Year more fun and feel less restrictive. A consultation with a personal organizer might be your answer.

4. Review your Key Life Sectors list. Are all these sectors relevant in your life at this time? If not, make any necessary changes or adjustments. In a 4 Personal Year, sometimes it is necessary to cut back on certain activities, and focus on essentials. The key is to be well organized.

5. This is a foundation year. Evaluate how you use your time. Use a weekly planner. Learn how to manage your time efficiently. Eliminate time and energy wasters. You will need all your attention to focus on achieving your goals this year. Implement a system that will help you organize your priorities. Stick to your Key Life Sectors and your goals for the year.

6. Note if there are any areas in your life in which you are overly rigid. If the 4 energy is already strong in your numbers, you may need to learn to relax a bit, maintain a positive and flexible attitude, and not lose track of your responsibilities toward others.

7. Go for a physical checkup if you haven't had one in a while. Establish healthy diet and exercise habits. Do a financial checkup. Make sure your budget is up to date and reflects your current situation and needs.

Exercise: Year-End Review
Complete this exercise at the end of your 4 Personal Year.

1. In what ways did you get organized and focused this year?

2. How has this added structure improved your life?

3. What is the most important lesson you learned this year?

4. What new knowledge will you bring into your upcoming 5 Personal Year?

The 4 Personal Year Goal Setting and Planning Worksheet

As an aid to your yearly planning, complete the following worksheet. Set goals for each of your Key Life Sectors. The 4 Personal Year is a foundation year, so you should be aiming for concrete results. Your efforts now will have an impact on the overall success of your current epicycle. Review your goals from last year. Do you need to make adjustments? Review your long-term goals. If you feel as though you are overwhelmed with responsibilities, rid yourself of clutter. Your goals should reflect your values and desires at this time of your life.

Goal Setting and Planning Worksheet My 4 Personal Year Dedication, Focus, Organization	
Key Life Sectors	*Goals for the year*
1	i
	ii
	iii
2	i
	ii
	iii
3	i
	ii
	iii
4	i
	ii
	iii
5	i
	ii
	iii
6	i
	ii
	iii

EIGHT

Freedom, Change, Progress

THE 5 PERSONAL YEAR

The stabilizing force of the number 4 gets a little shaking up as you move forward into the 5 Personal Year. If you were to continue with the same demanding pace, it wouldn't be long before you found yourself entrenched in a rut of work, duty, and obligation. Over time, your interest would fade, you would lose all sense of enthusiasm, grow bored, and probably become resentful of your limitations. The addition of a 1 to the 4 changes that. In the 5 Personal Year, it's time to do a little dance and break up the routine. It's a bit like adding a fifth leg to the table, only this leg is longer. You lose your balance, and anything can happen.

Fatigue, pressures from overwork, and feelings of restriction can build up in a 4 Personal Year, so that the energy of the 5 Year is usually quite welcome. It is often experienced as an increased desire for freedom, a need to loosen the holds of daily habits, and a yearning for change. This is a great year for travel and for making new acquaintances. Try to keep some free time in your weekly schedule so you can occasionally break away from the routine.

Your readiness for change as well as your need for change will determine the direction you will take this year. The years during which most major changes occur are the 1, 5, and 9 Personal Years. For each of these years, change is based on unique motivations, the 1 representing a renewal of energy and new beginnings, the 5 expressing a need for freedom and adventure, and the 9 manifesting completion and release. Common events for a 5 Personal Year include important job changes, relocations, home and family moves, and a change of orientation in school.

If you are comfortable with change, that is, if you have a healthy relationship with the energy of the number 5, you will enjoy the expansion and release from the containment and frustrations of last year. Your creativity will be unleashed and you will look for original ways of doing your work and reaching your goals. You will be ready for adventure and new experiences, ready to stretch yourself and do things you have never done before. This is the time to inject new elements or new activities into your ongoing projects.

If, on the other hand, you are not comfortable with the energy of the 5, if you have strong 4s or 2s for example, and prefer to hold on to old ways of doing things, you may find this year to be uncomfortably destabilizing. There is always an element of uncertainty in times of change, and whenever 5 energy is present, there are few guarantees, and often unexpected surprises can arise. No matter how solid your plan is, you cannot completely control the outcome of your choices. Sometimes, however, the injection of a new approach or new experience, even if it isn't sought out or even desired, is just what is needed to help move things forward in ways you could not have imagined. Without change, you could miss out on important opportunities for growth and progress.

Review your long-term goals. You are halfway through the current epicycle. Make those changes that will get you significantly closer to your goals. If you established a solid foundation last year, you should be in a good position to leap forward and take certain risks. This is a great time to promote yourself and your business. Expand your boundaries. Explore new avenues. In a 5 Personal Year, you can benefit from the right mix of flexibility, risk, and focus. Risk and flexibility will help you explore options that you might not otherwise consider, while a clear focus on your long-term goals will help move you forward with purpose and direction.

The 5 energy is quite progressive, and you could find yourself coming up with ideas that are a bit ahead of their time. You may have to practice patience until the world around you is ready for your bold new ideas. Although you may feel ready to try new ways of doing things, avoid leaping before thinking. The 5 can indicate a tendency for exaggeration, inconsistency, and impulsiveness. Don't lose track of your responsibilities and your long-term vision. Trying new things doesn't necessarily require that you throw out the baby with the bath water.

This is a much freer energy than the 4. You could encounter the breaking up of old conditions in your life, causing the delays and limitations of the past year to slowly dissipate. Some people respond to the energy of the 5 Personal Year by giving in to long-repressed restlessness, by moving, changing jobs, or changing interests or even love relationships without giving a second thought to the consequences of their actions. Be careful not to jump ship midstream. Change for the sake of change alone can set you back rather than forward. If change is not welcome, it can be a hectic and chaotic year. If you are ready for something new, it can be an exciting year.

Your success this year will depend on your ability to make wise choices, to flow with the changing conditions of your life, to release the old and accept the new, to be adventurous and ready to take some risks, all the while keeping your long-term goals in focus. Be aware of a tendency to overindulge in the good things—food, alcohol, and sensual pleasures. By maintaining balance, this can be a very enjoyable and fruitful year.

This is a great time for adventure and fun activities. In his 5 Personal Year, Bob, 52 and single, decided it was time to venture out and start dating. He was not interested in doing the bar scene, but some of the guys at work recommended that he try Internet dating. It was not something he would normally have done, yet, intrigued by the idea, he ventured out. This was a very exciting and rewarding time for Bob, where he learned much about dating and women, but more importantly, about himself.

Freedom from the weight of heavy responsibility doesn't always come in a happy package. If you will recall from the previous chapter, in a 4 Personal Year Denise was quite heavily burdened by the care of her ailing husband. In April of the following year, a 5 Personal Year of sudden change and a 9 Personal Month of endings and release, her husband suffered a severe stroke. Forty-eight hours later, he passed away. Understandably, this was a time of profound sorrow, a most traumatic moment in her life. Even though her husband had been seriously ill, she had never given up hope that he might get better. The stroke was unexpected and sudden, a typical 5 expression. This was also a time of liberation—now she was free of her responsibilities as full-time nurse and caretaker.

The expansiveness of the 5 energy also made this a time of much new learning for Denise, as she was plunged headfirst into the world of notaries, legal papers, taxes, finances, and sorting through the complex matters of settling her husband's estate. Later on that year, she was given her first computer and Internet account, adding even more new experiences as she was shown how to surf the Internet and collect her e-mail. In many ways, the radical energy of this 5 Personal Year pushed Denise to tap into her 3 Life Path skills like no other year before ever had.

The 5 Personal Year Month by Month

Note that the following descriptions for the Personal Months are to be used as guidelines for determining possible scenarios. Use the keywords from chapter 1 to interpret potential trends that apply to your particular lifestyle. Each person is unique, and each has a unique relationship with the numbers. Also keep in mind that the Personal Month trends are secondary to the Personal Year trends, and should be considered along with your Life Path and Birth Date numbers as well as your current Personal Year number.

JANUARY (6 Personal Month): Relationships, Home and Family

You are no doubt anxious to break free from the limitations and restrictions of last year. A 5 Personal Year can be an exciting time, with new opportunities just around the corner. Others sense this about you, and come to you for advice, or just for the pleasure of participating in joint projects. As you bring change into your life, especially home and family life, remember to do so in moderation. Others may not be ready for as much change as you are. Try to break up your routine with a little variety. Consider making your workspace more ergonomic. This is a good month to develop new personal and business relationships. Being at the start of a 5 Year, you will value your freedom more than usual, and may resent some of the responsibilities that restrict your movement.

FEBRUARY (7 Personal Month): Reflection, Meditation, Evaluation

Before things get too hectic, it might be a good idea to take some time out and review your situation, reevaluate your goals, both long-term and short-term, and make sure you have a solid plan in place. Your restlessness for change and adventure may conflict with your need to reflect. Try to find a balance between both urges; both are necessary for your growth and development. Take advantage of this introspective time to look for new ideas through inner guidance. Deepen your understanding of your life purpose and direction. You may not be open to the input of others this month, preferring to rely on your own insights. Even though you may be certain that you are right, you will have more support and cooperation in the long run if you remain sensitive and diplomatic.

MARCH (8 Personal Month): Money, Business, Finances

Business and money take precedence over other areas of activity this month. Your focus should be on expanding and pushing your professional goals forward. However, use wisdom in making financial choices. Do your due diligence, obtain proper advice before investing money and assets. If in doubt, wait. Avoid acting on impulse, especially when under a number 5 influence. Your excessive enthusiasm could cloud your judgment. Be patient in all financial matters. Your intuition could provide you with important insights as to how to inject new energy into your business. You are feeling quite dynamic now, and ready to explore new avenues. Again, this is not a great month for family and romance.

APRIL (9 Personal Month): Endings, Completion, Release

This can be an emotional time, with projects coming to a close and a sense of urgency to finish things off. In a 5 Personal Year, you are eager for change and new experiences, but the 9 Month requires that you first release any redundant or outdated activities and preoccupations from your life. A relationship that has caused you to feel restricted may come to an end. If the 5 energy is strong in your core numbers, you may be inclined to quit a project before it is completed, just to be relieved of its burden. Think twice about bringing something to an end before you have learned its lesson. Remember it is always best to earn your way out; that way you will never doubt your decision. This is a good time to travel and take a vacation.

MAY (1 Personal Month): Renewal, Progress, Promotion

This is a great time to promote yourself, your interests, or your business. Progress is easily accomplished now, and you are ready for new ideas and approaches. Use your creativity, ingenuity, and dramatic flare to get your point across, make a sale, or obtain support to get an innovative project underway. An excellent career move or opportunity is possible. This is the time to be bold and daring and to break away from old, worn-out ways of doing things. You could make an exciting new acquaintance this month. If you are single, get out there and make yourself known. Try something new and different. If in a relationship, be mindful of casual flirtations; instead, put some romance back into your marriage. Be adventurous.

JUNE (11/2 Personal Month): Sensitivity, Intuition, Relationships

Bursting with great ideas, you can derive much satisfaction by helping others with their new projects or with problem solving. You enjoy the company of colleagues and friends, especially those with whom you have shared interests. Your intuition is right on the mark and you could pick up on some interesting, innovative solutions for unexpected problems. However, be cautious with financial dealings. Your idealism and perhaps naïveté, if so inclined, may lead you in the wrong direction. There is a certain tension inside of you, an eagerness to produce something of importance. You have big dreams and you feel the need to share these with someone you trust. Open up and experience the closeness and comfort of sharing. Spend some time with someone you love; do something different.

JULY (3 Personal Month): Joie de Vivre, Travel, Socializing

This will probably be a very enjoyable month, an ideal time for a vacation, a road trip with family and friends. At work or in business, there will be plenty of opportunities for socializing and making great new contacts. Even though many businesses are on summer break, take advantage of this upbeat trend to enjoy leisure and fun activities with prospective clients and business acquaintances. Why not take up tennis or sailing? Join a cycling group; sign up for a golf tournament. Fortune shines on you; you might very well be in the right place at the right time. If you have a creative outlet, channel some of your inspiration into this activity. Use your talents now, they will serve you well. Take advantage of opportunities to communicate and promote your business.

AUGUST (13/4 Personal Month): Work, Work, Work

Well, it's time to pay the piper! Hopefully, you took some time off to rest and enjoy yourself last month. You'll have to get serious and attend to those details and work matters that you have been putting off for a while now. This is not a good month for a vacation! If you refuse to accept the work that is in front of you, you could be shortchanging yourself in the future. This is a foundation and bottom-line month. Focus on the important issues, the details, most likely those activities or tasks you've been cleverly avoiding. You can't ignore them forever! Make healthy and positive changes in your dietary and exercise habits. Take care of business on the home front. Work on those pesky little home projects that have been hanging around a long time.

SEPTEMBER (14/5 Personal Month): Freedom, Change, Surprises

If you worked hard last month, you will be rewarded with very interesting and exciting opportunities for growth and change. Always with your long-term plan in mind, explore new opportunities and prepare for change. If you have an abundance of number 5 energy among your numbers, you could be inclined to excessive restlessness and impatience or overindulging in food and drink. This month requires that you be flexible and open to change and new experiences, while keeping your eye on the ball. New relationships begun now may not be sustained in the long term. Release the old, go with the new, but use good judgment in all matters. Avoid making hasty decisions. Change for the sake of change alone may not be wise.

OCTOBER (6 Personal Month): Responsibility, Family, Balance

Family matters come to the fore as the 6 Personal Year approaches. If, despite your best efforts, you experienced excesses or veered off track last month, now is the time to pull yourself together and reestablish balance in your life. Enjoy the support, caring, and nurturing of family and friends. Plan a family get-together. Focus on diet and exercise. You may feel the crunch of added responsibility, especially from new projects or areas of activity that have recently been brought into your life. You will find pleasure in being helpful to others. A new acquaintance could bring much joy into your life. Prepare for a more moderate pace of life coming in the new year.

NOVEMBER (16/7 Personal Month): Reflection, Meditation, Analysis

It's time to take a serious look at where you have been, where you are, and where you are going. You may not be ready for such intense introspection, following a year of freedom, change, and opportunity. Perhaps you feel somewhat isolated, or different, as though others don't really understand you. Taking the time out to reflect could bring you much inner growth. Do research or background work. Make certain you are properly informed about the new areas of activity you have taken on in recent months. Reconnect with your inner guidance. Is the direction of your life in tune with your innermost desires? Are you living your passion? Are you pursuing your true life purpose? You may feel a little reclusive this month. Stay in tune with the needs of loved ones.

DECEMBER (8 Personal Month): Accomplishment, Power, Business

An exciting new business opportunity that might help move your career interests forward could present itself. Your focus is more on money and business than on family and leisure. Keep in mind that the 6 Personal Year is just a step away, so it will be important that you establish balance between career and personal life. Make choices and changes that will favor harmony in your lifestyle. You've had enough adventure and excitement this year to keep you motivated a while! You are more confident and empowered than you have been in a long time. This is a great period of personal accomplishment. You could be rewarded for a job well done. Money matters and finances are favored. A business acquaintance could provide you with a great new opportunity.

The 5 Personal Year Workshop

Complete this workshop at the beginning of the year along with your yearly planning and goal setting.

1. Relative to your Life Path, Birth Day number, and your personal experience of the number 5, are you ready to stretch yourself, be adventurous, and take on new challenges? If you are a strong 4, for example, you may find it difficult to deal with the unexpected occurrences and surprises that are common in a 5 Personal Year.

2. Go back to the last time you experienced a 5 Personal Year. What was going on in your life at that time? What changes did you make? Did you experience chaos, or measured progress and growth?

3. Relative to where you are in your life at this time, where would you like to see progress and growth? If you've had difficulty managing change in the past, how will you approach change now? How can you introduce change while maintaining an eye on your goals? How will change bring you closer to your goals?

4. Review your Key Life Sectors list. Are all these sectors relevant in your life at this time? Where would you like to make the most changes?

5. In what ways could you stretch yourself now, by trying something new, doing something different? Keep in mind that new experiences keep the brain healthy and the spirit youthful. What new skills would you like to learn?

6. While making changes, experimenting, and enjoying adventure, keep an eye on your long-term goals. Ensure continued progress in the right direction by aligning your actions with your values and your goals. Use creative and original ways of setting goals, such as maintaining a storyboard or scrapbook with pictures representing each of your goals.

7. If you are inclined to making radical decisions, take a deep breath, and think things through. Do your due diligence in all risky ventures. Are these changes appropriate? Are they necessary? Will they move you closer to your long-term goals? What will be the impact of these changes on your personal life? Your family life? Your professional life?

Exercise: Year-End Review

Complete this exercise at the end of your 5 Personal Year.

1. In what ways did your life change this year? How did you stretch yourself, expand your field of experience?

2. What are the benefits of these changes?

3. What is the most important lesson you learned this year?

4. What new knowledge will you bring into your upcoming 6 Personal Year?

The 5 Personal Year Goal Setting and Planning Worksheet

As an aid to your yearly planning, complete the following worksheet. Set goals for each of your Key Life Sectors. In a 5 Personal Year, you may crave a need for freedom. Look for ways of releasing some of your more restrictive duties and responsibilities; free up time to do fun or new things, while keeping an eye on your long-term goals. This can be a critical time for some, where the temptation to quit runs high, especially if they are feeling overwhelmed by last year's restrictions. Your goals should reflect your values and desires at this time of your life.

Goal Setting and Planning Worksheet My 5 Personal Year Freedom, Change, Progress	
Key Life Sectors	*Goals for the year*
1	i
	ii
	iii
2	i
	ii
	iii
3	i
	ii
	iii
4	i
	ii
	iii
5	i
	ii
	iii
6	i
	ii
	iii

NINE

Harmony, Responsibility, Family

THE 6 PERSONAL YEAR

*

| 1 | 2 | 3 | 4 | 5 | 6 | 7 | 8 | 9 |

After the excitement and rapid progress of the 5 Personal Year, you may be ready to settle down, catch your breath, and perhaps even find your bearings if last year put you in a tailspin. The addition of a 1 to the 5 energy establishes a new level of balance and provides opportunities for increased rewards through service to others, career advancement, and improved personal health and inner peace.

The 6 Personal Year brings attention to family and home life, and in particular, to all your responsibilities for others, whether at home, in the community, or in the workplace. While people express their increased need for your attention and help, you benefit from the comfort and support of home and family. Above all else, this year it is important that you reestablish a sense of balance in your life, otherwise you could feel overwhelmed with the burden of responsibility. People may need you more than ever now. They call on your knowledge and expertise; they make demands on your emotional and personal resources, including time, energy, and money.

Although the 6 is a number of service and responsibility, it is important to balance the time you spend in the service of others so as not to grow resentful of the demands made upon you. If you have 6s among your core numbers, you may already have a tendency to do too much for others. If this is the case, then this may be a good time to learn that sometimes it's okay and even very healthy for all concerned to simply say no. In fact, doing too much for others can have the effect of taking power away from them, and they in turn can become resentful of your meddling, even if it is well intentioned.

If you lack 6 energy, you could become resentful of your increasing responsibilities. Be honest with yourself and with others; only make those promises you know you can keep. Often it is better to promise less and deliver more than to constantly make promises that are never kept. Honesty and integrity will go a long way toward solidifying relationships this year. Honor your commitments to others and you will receive their respect in return.

Relationships that were developed and nurtured in your previous 2 Personal Year could bear fruit now, and you may benefit from the protection and support of those whom you have served well in the past. During a 6 Personal Year, it is not uncommon to receive recognition from your peers or superiors for a job well done. You could become involved in teaching, coaching, counseling, advising, or mediating and peacemaking in work or domestic situations. While helping others resolve their problems, do not neglect your family and friends. At the same time, you do not need to be a martyr. Your keyword for the year should be balance, in all things.

Unlike last year, this is a year of moderate but steady growth and advancement. Focus on the issues that are close at hand. Complete projects and activities as they present themselves. Avoid procrastination. If you are well organized, settling into your roles and responsibilities should be relatively easy, and you will shine in your function, especially if you have a management role. Take care of settling bills, banking, and estate matters, as well as long-term financial plans this year.

You will feel the need for close, personal relationships, and if single, you could find love knocking at your door. Your nesting urge could kick in and you may want to start a family. Settling down, getting married, and attending to the details of everyday life has a certain appeal now. This is a time for consolidating personal relationships and for emotional grounding. It is an excellent year for marriage, love, and romance. If you have some unresolved issues in a personal relationship, now would be a good time to get some help in the form of counseling, or to do some reading on the subject of relationships.

You will seek and enjoy giving and receiving affection. You strive for balance, harmony, serenity, and beauty in your surroundings as well as in your relationships. Home or domestic responsibilities require your attention, and you could buy or rent a home, renovate a property, buy furniture, paint, or decorate. Consult a feng shui expert to bring more harmony in your home and work environments.

If you think a normal happy family is not for you, keep in mind that when the timing is right, things somehow manage to fall into place. Peter came to see me when he was 25 years old, in a 9 Personal Year. His charts indicated a sensitive, caring personality, typical of a 2 Life Path person. He had tremendous potential for working with people, in a counseling capacity or in the community in areas such as social work or police work. At the time, all these options seemed to be closed to him. He supported himself with a full-time job in shipping, had debts to pay off, and no family he could call on for help. Not academically inclined, and with only a high school diploma, higher education was out of the question. In his youth, he had gotten into trouble with drugs and the law. He was a recovering addict, and had a criminal record. By all appearances, social work and police work were out of the question. Yet he knew that his job was unsatisfactory, and in the long run he would have to find something more fulfilling.

I studied his charts for some idea of how he might express some of his talents, even in a minor way, so that at the end of the day he would feel a certain degree of satisfaction. It's not given to every person to find complete fulfillment in their day job. Sometimes, a job is simply necessary for survival, a means to an end. Many people find contentment in their personal life, in their function as caregivers for family and friends, through some form of creative self-expression, or through involvement in the community.

Peter had some clear talents and abilities, but appeared to be faced with nothing but closed doors. I could see that he wouldn't be happy in the long run in his current situation, even if he did move up the ranks and acquire more authority or management responsibilities. During our conversation, he expressed having a dream of working with adolescents who had trouble with drugs and the law, much as he had experienced a few years earlier. Looking for a way for him to tap into his natural inclinations and stir up feelings of personal satisfaction, I suggested that he volunteer a few hours a week at a local youth support organization. That way, I explained, he would be using some of his talents and satisfying a very real and unexpressed need to help others, the natural expression of his 2 Life Path.

Peter phoned me just before Christmas, two years later. By then he was at the end of a 2 Personal Year. Shyly, he mentioned his name, asking if I remembered him. Of course, I did. How could I forget such a remarkably kind and caring young man? He had called to tell me that he had taken my advice and found volunteer work with a youth group downtown. He had volunteered with this group for eighteen months, at which point, given his natural ability for the work, the director offered him a full-time position. At an age where most youth are out partying and having a good time, facing seemingly insurmountable obstacles, this young man followed his heart, put himself in the flow of his natural talents and abilities, and caused the tide of opportunities to turn in his favor. A few years later, in the 6 Personal Year, he found love, married, and had his first child. By putting himself on his true path, he aligned himself with the opportunities that flowed as natural consequences of his actions.

It sometimes takes tremendous courage and faith in yourself to actively pursue the dreams you were born to follow. They don't have to be big dreams, as in the case of this young man. He's not likely to become a millionaire on a social worker's salary, but he is following his true purpose and he is making and will continue to make a difference in the lives of many troubled young souls.

After being plunged into a series of adventures and new experiences in her 5 Personal Year, Denise, whose story we began in the chapter on the 4 Personal Year, received a call for help from her sister. In her 6 Personal Year, Denise made several trips to a town three hours away to help her sister following leg and arm surgery that left her incapable of taking care of herself. With her help, her sister recovered remarkably well. The 6 often requires that you set your own needs aside for the sake of others.

Although the 6 Year is generally experienced as positive, favoring home and family relationships, if you have some unresolved issues with family or if you have not come to terms with your responsibilities toward others, this can be a difficult year. Ivan, a highly sensitive 11/2 Life Path with a strong sense of specialness, found himself out of work in his 6 Personal Year. Unable to see himself as a member of the mainstream career track, he failed to connect with the opportunities that came his way. Job interviews invariably ended the same way: either he was overqualified for the job or underexperienced. His wife was pressuring him to get a job and pull his weight. They had lost their home and were living in a relative's house. During that year, Ivan could not see beyond his own specialness and failed to sacrifice his needs for those of his wife and daughter, creating additional tension. It was a very unsettling time during which he lost not only his job, but he also nearly lost his marriage. Unlike Peter, Ivan was unable to set aside his needs and thus could not benefit from the normally supportive and protective influences of the number 6.

The 6 Personal Year Month by Month

Note that the following descriptions for the Personal Months are to be used as guidelines for determining possible scenarios. Use the keywords from chapter 1 to interpret potential trends that apply to your particular lifestyle. Each person is unique, and each has a unique relationship with the numbers. Also keep in mind that the Personal Month trends are secondary to the Personal Year trends, and should be considered along with your Life Path and Birth Date numbers as well as your current Personal Year number.

JANUARY (7 Personal Month): Reflection, Analysis, Study

As the new year begins, you will want to spend a little more time than usual on your yearly planning and goal setting. Above all, you realize that your life cannot continue at the same pace it did in the last year. Your key goal this year should be to establish balance and harmony in all aspects of your life. It may seem boring at first glance, but you will benefit by doing all things in good measure. You may feel a little lost right now, as the energy of the previous year winds down. You'll need some alone time this month, so take some time out, read, meditate, take a spa weekend, or go for long walks in the woods. Do not worry if things are not moving as quickly as you expect them to. They won't move as fast as last year, but they will move, in time. Think about how you might improve on your home and family life this year.

FEBRUARY (8 Personal Month): Power, Business, Money

Your attention will be on business, money, and career matters this month. Significant results may be achieved now. You are in an excellent position to receive recognition for a job well done. Long-standing professional relations can lead to further opportunities for advancement. If you are remembering to keep a balance between home and work, you will be able to share your achievements with family members. Tend to money matters relating to home and property. Invest in that renovation project you've been putting off. Put money aside for a family vacation later this year. Although the 6 Personal Year doesn't normally indicate big flashy accomplishments, this can be a very productive month.

MARCH (9 Personal Month): Generosity, Completion, Endings

Determine which of your responsibilities are appropriate at this point in your current epicycle. If you have strong 6 energy in your core numbers, you may be in the habit of taking on way more responsibility than is necessary or even healthy. People sense this, and can take advantage of your giving nature. Sometimes, you are not doing a person a favor by doing for them what they can be taught to do for themselves. This may be a good time for a relationship cleanup. On the other hand, you may be drawn to participate in a community or volunteer project. Your heart reaches out to others, and you are in a giving and expansive mood. In all interactions with others, patience, compassion, and understanding are called for. Keep in mind that this is a month of endings; complete or unload unfinished projects.

APRIL (1 Personal Month): Initiative, Relationships, Renewal

Begin new home projects or plan an activity with family members. Your loved ones will appreciate your upbeat and energetic attitude, and you will enjoy the time spent with them. Proceed with confidence and initiative with your plans. Money, career, and personal advancement are favored. You may be ready for marriage or an engagement. Consider renewing your vows with your existing partner. If you are in a difficult relationship in which issues have not been successfully worked out, you may be ready to move on. You feel lucky, positive, and supported. Your leadership skills can be put to good use in a team project. If you are single and seeking companionship, you might meet someone special. Stir some romance into your love life.

MAY (11/2 Personal Month): Intuition, Idealism, Inspiration

The pace slows down a bit this month. You may have to wait while new projects begun last month take shape. Your intuition guides you in your dealings with family and close friends, and you may be called on to settle a misunderstanding or dispute. Your heightened sensitivity and desire for harmony allow you to find positive solutions for all concerned. Fully appreciative of your valued relationships, you find reward and comfort in domestic activities. Remain patient and allow things to develop in their own time. Avoid arguments and disputes—you may be too emotionally involved to be objective. Use tact and diplomacy in all interactions. You could benefit from inner guidance if you are open and receptive.

JUNE (3 Personal Month): Self-Expression, Creativity, Enjoyment

You will be in the mood to socialize, go out with friends, have a good time, and generally take advantage of this early summer month with fun activities. This is an excellent time for a family vacation. Even if you must work, schedule some weekend road trips, enjoy the surrounding scenery, take in an outdoor concert, play softball or golf, go strawberry picking. You could be easily distracted, so keep your calendar flexible. At the same time, be aware of a tendency for spending money. Luck is on your side now, and your upbeat and positive attitude makes you a delight to be with. This is a time for romance. A new relationship could be blossoming nicely. Taking time out for artistic or creative projects could also be very rewarding. Have fun and enjoy yourself this month.

JULY (13/4 Personal Month): Work, Service, Discipline

Hopefully, you didn't become overly distracted last month, because now you will need to get back to work. This is certainly not the best time for rest and relaxation. You seem to be pulled in two directions with a need to pay attention to a pile of work at home on the one hand, and another healthy load in your job or business. Being organized in all areas of your life will make the work much easier to handle. Finish projects around the home, while attending to the details of work. If you are working on a renovation project, you could encounter some challenges. Maintain a positive attitude, even though you would probably rather be doing anything else but work. Spend time with family, even if you don't have time for a vacation this month. This is a very productive month for work.

AUGUST (14/5 Personal Month): Change, Surprises, Freedom

You may be feeling the need for a little escape and adventure this month. Many responsibilities have been added to your task list this year, and you could use a little breathing room. Enjoy activities with family; do those new and unusual things you've been planning on doing but never got around to doing. This is an excellent period for social activities, for a vacation, and for meeting new people. In order to give yourself a little free time, delegate some of those less interesting responsibilities. If you can't delegate, then, if possible, just let them go for the time being. Be flexible and remain prepared to accommodate surprises. This can be an excellent month for promoting yourself or your business. Try new approaches; be bold and daring; experiment. Sometimes, change is as good as a rest.

SEPTEMBER (6 Personal Month): Harmony, Family, Home

You will enjoy time spent with family and friends this month, and especially activities centered on the home. If you haven't established order and balance in your life, you may feel somewhat restricted by all the responsibilities that seem to be coming at you from every direction. You may even feel resentful of those who seem to make too many demands on your time and energy. If your lifestyle is balanced, you will enjoy getting involved in some community activity or family project. Devote yourself to the needs of others; set your own needs aside for the time being. You will be rewarded for your dedication and service. This is a good month for money and business. Tend to your health. Take a day off work and go to a spa.

OCTOBER (7 Personal Month): Analysis, Reflection, Isolation

With all the extra focus on service to others this year, you probably feel that you've earned a little time out just for you! Pick up the latest novel, meditate, go for long walks in the woods, or go fishing. Schedule a spa weekend. Reflect on the progress you've made so far; review the goals you set back in January. Adjust these goals to better suit any new developments that may have occurred over the past couple of months, if necessary. Consider your personal, home, family, and career goals for the future. The 7 Personal Year is next, bringing attention on the inner life, reflection, and solitary activities. Inner healing and growth will be your new focus. For now, look for ways of improving family life. Your deep insights can be very helpful in resolving long-standing issues.

NOVEMBER (8 Personal Month): Career, Money, Business

This is an excellent time for business and money matters, the culmination of your efforts of the closing year. You could make an important decision regarding a home or family matter. You have learned much about balancing home and career, and are ready to implement measures that will ensure continued harmony for all concerned. This is a rewarding time, when results are finally manifesting in a tangible fashion. Tend to financial affairs, especially as they relate to home and family. You could be contemplating the future of your business as you approach the start of a 7 Personal Year. Keep in mind that the current epicycle will peak in just over a year, the 8 Personal Year. Focus on tangible results.

DECEMBER (9 Personal Month): Completion, Endings, Release

Finish those long-standing home projects, clean out the garage, feng shui your home, relieve yourself of clutter. Do whatever it takes to ensure harmony and peacefulness in your home and work environments. Next year, you will have lots of things on your mind, and you won't want to be bothered by material details. This is a 9 Month of endings, not the time to begin major new undertakings. While you allow the year to wind down naturally, focus your attention on a community or charitable activity. A relationship that has served its purpose may come to an end. You may feel a little emotional, or uncertain as you part ways. Take a family vacation, bring your family to the beach, and get some much-needed rest.

The 6 Personal Year Workshop

Complete this workshop at the beginning of the year along with your yearly planning and goal setting.

1. Relative to your Life Path, Birth Day number, and your personal experience of the number 6, how do you feel about your responsibilities toward those who are close to you? Is there love, peace, and harmony in your life?

2. Go back to the last time you experienced a 6 Personal Year. What was going on in your personal and professional life at that time? Were you at peace? Was there balance in your personal and professional relationships? Were you able to receive the support you needed from others to accomplish your goals?

3. Relative to where you are in your life at this time, how would you like to see your relationships improved? For example, if you are a freedom-loving 5 Life Path, how could you be more responsible? Or more balanced? If you are a deep-thinking and solitary 7 Life Path, consider how your solitary nature has affected your ability to build strong personal relationships. If you are a career-focused 8 Life Path, how can you bring more balance into your life?

4. Review your Key Life Sectors list. Are all these sectors still relevant at this time? If not, make any necessary changes or adjustments. Is there one area that needs more balance than others? Work on establishing balance between the various areas your life.

5. Is there time in your hectic schedule for peaceful, healing, creative, or harmonious activities such as yoga or listening to music? Spending some time on an artistic project can have a very soothing effect on the soul. The key to a successful 6 Personal Year is to establish a sense of peacefulness in your life, regardless of how crazy things may appear.

6. Put a little romance back into your life. This may be challenging, especially if you and your partner have grown apart over the past few years. Go out on dates where you pretend that you don't know each other. You may be surprised at how much you and your partner have changed. Become reacquainted. You could set your relationship on a whole new course.

7. If you tend to be overinvolved in the affairs of others, how can you be more respectful of personal boundaries? Meddling can cause resentment. What do you fear you will lose if you pull away a bit and establish more healthy boundaries? Get counseling if this is a challenge for you.

Exercise: Year-End Review

Complete this exercise at the end of your 6 Personal Year.

1. In what ways did you bring more balance and harmony into your life?

2. What are the benefits from this increased balance?

3. What is the most important lesson you learned this year?

4. What new knowledge will you bring into your upcoming 7 Personal Year?

The 6 Personal Year Goal Setting and Planning Worksheet

As an aid to your yearly planning, complete the following worksheet. Set goals for each of your Key Life Sectors. In a 6 Personal Year, you should seek to achieve balance and harmony in all aspects of your life. Tend to your responsibilities. Release those duties that are really beyond your scope. Your goals should reflect your values and desires at this time of your life.

Goal Setting and Planning Worksheet My 6 Personal Year Harmony, Responsibility, Family	
Key Life Sectors	*Goals for the year*
1	i
	ii
	iii
2	i
	ii
	iii
3	i
	ii
	iii
4	i
	ii
	iii
5	i
	ii
	iii
6	i
	ii
	iii

TEN

✦ ✦ ✦

Reflection, Analysis, the Inner Life

THE 7 PERSONAL YEAR

As a counterbalance to the pull of responsibilities and relationships of last year, the addition of a 1 to the 6 generates the unusual and sometimes challenging energy of the 7 Personal Year. You are now in the third and final phase of your 9-Year Epicycle. The 7 year brings a period of temporary withdrawal from the hustle and bustle of worldly and material existence. Seven is the number of the inner life. It requires that you get in touch with your innermost values and desires, which can put you at odds with the generally more materialistic standards of the world around you.

Your current epicycle has no doubt built up significant momentum by now, and you may be ready for a break. I like to call the 7 Year the "calm before the storm," except that *storm* carries such negative connotations. It's a period of regrouping, while you gather your inner strength and resources to be better prepared to go all out in your big 8 Personal Year coming next year. Although no one really likes to slow down, you need this time out to catch your breath and refocus on your goals.

One of the purposes of this period of reflection is to allow you the opportunity to fully digest and integrate the lessons acquired through your experiences to date. The better you understand yourself and the way you respond to life situations, the more likely you will be to make the most of your upcoming trends. This is a year of introspection, analysis, and seclusion. This is a good time for studies, especially if additional learning will give you the skill set you need to be in a better position to take advantage of rising opportunities.

This is the ideal time to take up any activity that requires a certain degree of quiet and solitude. Although you will continue to pursue your daily activities as before, you will have a greater need than usual for moments of seclusion. Take long, hot baths in the evening, set time aside to read inspirational or self-help books or listen to recordings, get up early in the morning and go for long walks in the park, do a half-hour of yoga, tai chi, meditation, or deep-breathing exercises, or get involved in an intensive fitness program. Your best strategy now is to turn your focus inward. Running about and pursuing material goals will bring less satisfaction, lead to fewer results, and could also prove to be destructive.

In fact, in a 7 Personal Year, pursuing material goals alone can be counterproductive. Andrea, a hard-working 13/4 Life Path financial advisor, experienced an intense period of self-questioning during her 7 Personal Year. With several years of dedicated hard work behind her, she had reached a certain level of success in her position. However, she felt that she would not reach her full potential unless she made a career move. She pursued several avenues during that year, went on many job interviews, but nothing worked out. For Andrea, money was one of the major issues. There was never enough to justify a job change.

In September of that year, a 16/7 Month of intense analysis and introspection, once again she was faced with a couple of career options. Again, the position she really wanted fell short of her desired salary range. Since she was in a 16/7 Month, I suggested she take money out of the equation and consider the job on its deeper merits. She gave it further thought, recognized that this was the best job given her talents and abilities and career goals, and decided to accept the position, despite the lower pay. To her surprise, the following day upper management reconsidered her salary demands, and she was given the amount she had originally wanted. Sometimes it pays to follow your heart rather than the money.

Not to worry, this period of withdrawal from the material world is temporary. You have not suddenly become an antisocial recluse. It's just that you need a bit of time out for yourself. Years of intensive focus on the outside, material world need to be balanced by introspection and nonmaterial concerns. Reevaluate your goals and long-term aspirations. Measure your progress. Ensure that your expectations for future accomplishments are realistic. After this year, only two years remain in the current epicycle. Learn to appreciate yourself, simply, as you are, not defined by the requirements of the outside world. Self-love is a valuable asset.

A friend of mine, a successful author, counselor, and businesswoman, a typical 8 Life Path woman, decided to plan a trip to El Camino for an upcoming 7 Personal Year. At first, I thought the idea sounded quite appropriate—a meditative, spiritual journey, quiet time spent in nature. Then the innate 8 Life Path energy kicked in (along with other 8s active at the time) and the project suddenly began to grow into a more impressive undertaking, including the writing of a journal for eventual publication. At that point, I started to think that although filled with incredible potential, the project seemed more appropriate for an 8 or even a 9 Personal Year. As it turned out, once the 7 Personal Year finally arrived, another opportunity surfaced, requiring a radical move and almost total seclusion to a small town in the country, a typical 7 environment. The El Camino adventure was postponed for another time.

It is not uncommon to experience feelings of specialness and superiority in a 7 period. A 7 Year can send certain individuals into a self-critical, overly analytical tailspin. The inward pull of the 7 energy can be difficult to handle, and you may have to struggle hard to keep from slipping into the clutches of negative thinking, loneliness, or even depression. Fighting against the natural trend toward introspection will only lead to feelings of frustration, confusion, and resentment.

A 7 Personal Year is typically not a year for manifesting great outward achievement. Progress generally remains below the surface, expressed more as a deepened understanding of self and of life. It may also manifest as a greater knowledge in your field of work or expertise. You will experience far more personal satisfaction at the end of the year if you have allowed yourself to develop a positive and healthy relationship with your inner life.

An Inner Life Journey

The following personal account is included here as it clearly illustrates the power and effectiveness of deep visualization techniques when applied to concrete life circumstances. Despite the popularity of books that teach the power of mind and focusing on intention, many people remain under the misguided impression that meditation is for highly evolved spiritual beings, or that creative visualization is for gifted mystics and not for everyone. Granted, I have spent some years exploring various spiritual disciplines, but the technique described below, derived from these experiences, is very simple and easy to use and requires no particular training in meditation techniques. All that is required is a desire to experience change, a willingness to do something about your current circumstances, and the ability to sit quietly for brief periods of time.

The events described below occurred during a particularly challenging time, a transition period covering a 9 and a 1 Personal Year. I was well into my 1 Personal Year when it occurred to me that it was time to take matters into my own hands and make some serious changes—clearly a number 1 influence. At the time, I lived in an apartment in the core of the city, surrounded by cement and asphalt, while I craved a garden and cedar hedge so badly it hurt inside. I was holding on to a job that I hated, desperately afraid of not being able to survive if I pursued my true life purpose.

My fear of letting go and moving forward, something that should have been accomplished in the 9 Personal Year, was unmistakably symbolized by the postinfectious polyneuritis I had sustained following a losing battle with a flu virus that fall. My body had become numb from my waist down to my toes. It no doubt sounds worse than it was; the condition didn't prevent me from walking or moving my legs, it only caused lack of sensation. The result was that I walked cautiously on spongy feet, and shaved my legs more slowly. It was, if anything, moderately annoying. I took this ailment as a symbol of my fear of walking on my true path.

The doctor had informed me, in a somewhat bland tone, that they didn't know everything about the workings of the spine and brain, and that the condition would probably remain permanent, a diagnosis that I found unacceptable. At the same time, I was struggling with early, probably stress-induced perimenopausal symptoms that included head-splitting migraines and a case of acne so severe that I would leave the apartment to shop for essentials in the evenings only, too embarrassed to be seen in the light of day. I took this particular symptom as a symbol of my reluctance to face my true self. And then there were the heart palpitations, which speak for themselves.

Having had my fill of setbacks and obstacles, I decided to take action, but first, I needed to look deep inside and see what was driving my life. In need of quick results, I modified an inner journey exercise I had learned years before, simplifying it to the bare essentials I felt would be appropriate for my current situation. I settled comfortably on my couch, legs crossed beneath me. I had made certain that I would not be disturbed, and the apartment was silent. A stick of Japanese temple incense and a candle burned nearby. Note that candles and incense are not a requirement for effective meditation, but they happen to be a part of the rituals I enjoy to set the mood.

With eyes closed, I focused my attention on the space behind my eyes, in the center of my head. From there, I visualized an elevator, which I took for the journey down to my core, which I pictured at the level of my pelvic girdle. I then left the elevator and entered a cavernlike chamber. I looked around for objects that might give me clues as to what was influencing me at the level of my foundation. The cavern was empty. Good sign, I thought. No objects, no foreign influences. Then I proceeded to find the exit of the cavern, over to the front and toward the left slightly. I headed outside, to the front of the cavern, to explore my path, in search of clues that might indicate why my life was so jammed up and what I might do to clear the way.

What a shock I experienced when I reached the start of my path! Normally, the path should be natural, like a footpath in the woods, clear of objects and people, for these are indicators of outside influences. Instead, what arose before me was literally the largest pile of garbage I had ever seen. It was as though refuse from the entire Island of Montreal had been dumped on my path. Shocked, but not surprised, I proceeded to take action. I understood that I had to consciously destroy all that was blocking my progress. I also knew that what lay on my path were my own unresolved issues, garbage from my life, matters I had not completely dealt with such as fear, insecurity, lack of confidence, and self-esteem issues.

Determined to clear the way, I strapped on the largest laser-firing bazooka I could imagine myself holding, and began to fire away. That's the fun part of creative visualization. You can allow yourself to imagine whatever works for you. Of course, I understood that it would take many excursions before the entire heap of waste was destroyed. As well, I would have to take measures in my physical life parallel to actions taken in my imagined inner life. But I was optimistic. I had found something that spoke to me, and I was determined to deal with it. Which is exactly what I did.

The first order of business was to terminate a very toxic relationship. Afterward, I gathered my courage and negotiated a leave from my job that allowed me to work as a contractor while rebuilding my consulting practice on the side. I accidentally (if there are truly accidents) rediscovered the Bach Flower Remedies when a book jutting out of its shelf space at my local homeopathic pharmacy caught my attention. These remedies helped take the edge off the deeper fears, insecurities, and lack of confidence.

Every once in a while, I would repeat the process, returning to my path, firing away additional rounds of ammunition. Month by month, the pile grew smaller and smaller. A little over a year later, nearly all physical symptoms had disappeared, including the polyneuritis. I cancelled my monthly appointments with the neurologist. I was also well on my way to building my consulting practice and I had purchased my first home, and, yes, it was surrounded by a cedar hedge and eventually had a large garden. A final journey to my inner self revealed a path that was clear of debris, made of soft, fine golden sand, winding gently before me, clearly symbolic of the new life that was defining itself before me.

This technique has served me well over the years, and has also helped many of my clients clear blockages of their own. It is simple to use, and doesn't require tremendous visualization ability. It can also be lots of fun. There is no law that says that self-development and inner healing can't be enjoyable!

The 7 Personal Year Month by Month

Note that the following descriptions for the Personal Months are to be used as guidelines for determining possible scenarios. Use the keywords from chapter 1 to interpret potential trends that apply to your particular lifestyle. Each person is unique, and each has a unique relationship with the numbers. Also keep in mind that the Personal Month trends are secondary to the Personal Year trends, and should be considered along with your Life Path and Birth Date numbers as well as your current Personal Year number.

JANUARY (8 Personal Month): Material Accomplishment, Business

As the 7 Personal Year is introspective in nature, this would be a good month to set up your agenda for the year in such a way as to give yourself more time for thought and reflection. Scheduling some personal time into your weekly agenda will be very beneficial. Focus on planning and goal setting for the next two to three years. This is a good month for all business activities. You have great ideas that can be turned into innovative projects in business or at work. You are getting a good sense of which of your projects you will be able to bring to completion as the current epicycle approaches its peak next year. You benefit from increased confidence and self-assurance. Questions bearing on the meaning of life may begin to pique your interest as you move forward toward achieving your material goals.

FEBRUARY (9 Personal Month): Completion, Endings, Giving

Projects that need to be completed this month keep you from the alone time you seek. You will need to be considerate of the feelings of others if you don't want to push people away. The stirrings of deep inner questioning may make you feel somewhat uncomfortable. You may wonder about the satisfaction you derive from your work, your relationships, or your lifestyle. After having built up a momentum over the past few years, working hard toward the accomplishment of your goals, you may find it disquieting to suddenly find yourself questioning all aspects of your life. You may feel overly emotional, easily irritated by the demands made by others. Release some of the activities or people that no longer serve a purpose in your life. Spend some time volunteering at your local community center. Wait for next month before making important changes.

MARCH (1 Personal Month): Originality, Self-Determination

This month marks the start of a complete 9-month cycle, indicating the potential for much inner growth and progress throughout the year. This is an excellent time to begin studies, meditation, or quiet reflective practices such as tai chi, yoga, or even gardening and reading. If you have been putting off a research or study project for later, now is the time to begin. Proceed with confidence with a challenging new project, something that you can sink your teeth into, or something that will force you to think, analyze, and work out complex issues. A 1 Personal Month in a 7 Personal Year is a time in which you will be particularly self-focused. Be aware of a tendency to be overly selfish, lest you hurt the ones who matter to you.

APRIL (11/2 Personal Month): Sharing, Joint Projects, Intuition

You will probably need to work closely with others this month, an experience that could cause you a bit of frustration, given that you are more inclined to do your own thing this year. This can be an intense month, during which you will be working hard at resolving complex problems but then not necessarily seeing immediate results. Patience in all areas, especially when working with others, is required. Be careful of a tendency of feeling superior or overly special. Remain focused on the task at hand. Your intuition is working overtime as you are motivated from deep within to pursue your interests. Inner guidance is a strong force and can provide you with valuable creative solutions to immediate problems.

A passing comment from a friend or acquaintance could help you know yourself better. Keep an open mind, and avoid making rash decisions.

MAY (3 Personal Month): Creativity, Enjoyment, Self-Expression

Although still in a reclusive year, you are inclined to socialize a bit this month, as you need a much-deserved break from all that introspection. Yet, even in your socializing you will be more interested in discussing serious topics than wasting time on superficial chitchat and gossip. The 7 Personal Year has begun to draw you deeper inside; you may be reflecting on the meaning of life, as well as your life purpose. You may find it difficult to pull yourself out of your inner musings and focus on the mundane. Be careful not to fall into excessive analysis and criticism this month. Focus on a quiet, enjoyable, creative task. You could enjoy journaling or participating in a book club or other discussion group. Use creative ways of exploring your inner self.

JUNE (13/4 Personal Month): Work, Focus, Dedication

As a means of returning to your seclusion, you won't mind being buried in hard work this month, especially if this work can be done alone. There is no way around it: you will have to attend to the details of day-to-day life, both at home and on the job. Avoid becoming impatient with trivial matters and details. This is a very productive month, so keep your nose to the grindstone, and you will accomplish much more than you ever thought possible. A well-organized routine will make the days go by more smoothly. Work with your weekly planner and manage your time efficiently. Stick to the task at hand. You could enjoy spending some time on a home or garden project. You are focused on yourself again; remember to reach out to close ones. Involve your spouse or children in a home project.

JULY (14/5 Personal Month): Surprises, Change, Expansion

And now for a complete change of pace! You might as well throw your agenda out the window—the next couple of weeks will be a little unpredictable and challenging to organize. Keep an open mind; unexpected news or events could cause you to rethink some of your plans. You could be feeling restless, anxious to get on with some of the ideas you've been mulling over these past few months. Unforeseen circumstances could intrude on your alone time, but that's okay. You need a little fun and excitement in your life right about now. Remain flexible so as not to grow frustrated if your agenda gets shuffled around. Your mind is keen and you are eager to explore new topics of interest. Able to think outside the box, you could find innovative solutions to long-standing problems. Focus on original approaches.

AUGUST (6 Personal Month): Family, Home Life, Balance

After last month's excitement, you will need a little balance in your routine. Even though you may be eager to return to doing your own thing, you will benefit greatly by spending time with family and close friends. Comfort and affection received from your partner will do wonders for your restless soul. Your relationship could deepen as a result of time well spent together. A 6 Personal Month is always a time for giving and receiving. Domestic responsibilities are your priority now. Establish an air of peace and harmony and you will enjoy your time at home. A family vacation to a quiet location would do you and your loved ones a world of good. Take some time out to listen to music, read, or enjoy your favorite hobby. Your creativity could flow smoothly.

SEPTEMBER (16/7 Personal Month): Analysis, Reflection, Isolation

This year you have spent much time in thought, and this month you may feel the need to withdraw even more. Guard against the tendency to overanalyze and to be overly critical of yourself or of others. You question everything, but be patient, for answers must come in their own time. Much personal growth is possible if you allow the inner transformation to occur naturally. This is an intense time, with much learning and an increased sense of self-awareness. This is not the time to plan a family vacation or important social or public events. If you feel yourself growing depressive, go for long walks in the woods, spend some time in the garden, or get in touch with nature. Find a confidant with whom to share your feelings and thoughts. Read an inspirational book.

OCTOBER (8 Personal Month): Business, Practical Awareness

You are now in a position to start applying much of what you have learned this year, whether about yourself, about life, or about your situation. You are in no mood for superficialities, and you have a no-nonsense approach to business, work, and money matters this month. Excellent progress can be made in business now. You have grown stronger in self-knowledge and understanding, and you are in a better position to make decisions that reflect your true life purpose. This causes you to rethink the goals you set for yourself several years ago. You are now preparing for an 8 Personal Year, during which you will have the opportunity to put it all together, finally accomplishing your goals. You could be feeling quite confident, and should definitely reward yourself for your efforts.

NOVEMBER (9 Personal Month): Completion, Release

Although you may have experienced feelings of uncertainty or maybe even confusion over the past few months, your self-awareness has no doubt increased tremendously. As the year comes to a close, this intense learning process is coming to an end. Soon you will begin to feel a deep relief. If you have attended to your inner life, you will have grown much. If you have resisted it and ignored its call, you could feel uncertain about your upcoming 8 Year. The 8 Personal Year is a year of harvest; as you have sown, so shall you reap. Your efforts of the past years will show concrete results. This can be frightening if you have ignored your duties and responsibilities to yourself and to others along the way. For the time being, let go, finish projects, and relax. Wait for the renewal of energy that the next month, a 1 Personal Month, will bring. Volunteer some time and energy with your preferred community organization. Focus on others rather than on yourself.

DECEMBER (1 Personal Month): Renewal, Initiative, Rebirth

Based on everything you have learned this year, you are probably ready to make some changes in your life. You've done a lot of thinking, and you have greater self-awareness now. Your energy level is up, and you feel invigorated and prepared to tackle any challenges the world might put on your path. You may be sensing that your big year is coming, and it is. Your focus is very much on yourself now, so don't forget to balance your day with time out for family and friends. Avoid making hasty decisions; the time is not quite right yet. Keep in mind that you are approaching the end of the epicycle, and any changes you implement now should contribute to bringing current projects to completion. Focus on short-term goals.

The 7 Personal Year Workshop

Complete this workshop at the beginning of the year.

1. Relative to your Life Path, Birth Day number, and your personal experience of the number 7, evaluate your ability to spend quality time alone. Are you comfortable reflecting, meditating, and turning inward for guidance? Are you able to connect with inner guidance when in need of direction?

2. Recall the last time you experienced a 7 Personal Year. What was going on in your life at that time? Were you attempting to forge ahead toward outward and material accomplishments, or did you respect your need for quiet and contemplation?

3. Relative to where you are in your life at this time, how can you improve on your connection with your inner self?

4. Review your Key Life Sectors list. Are all these sectors still relevant? Schedule some quiet time in your daily agenda. Take up yoga, meditation, or reading. Let others know that you need time for reflection. You don't have to be a savage recluse and alienate people in the process. Read inspirational books, listen to inspirational tapes or CDs, and watch inspirational videos. Spend some time enjoying the garden or walking in the woods.

5. Consider deepening your expertise, either personal or professional, through study, research, courses, or readings. Is there an area of your life that would benefit from additional studies or research? A 7 Year is an excellent time to hone your skills or develop an expertise.

6. Are there social responsibilities that could be cut back to allow you more personal quiet time? This is not the best time to chair a fundraising event! Focus on solitary activities.

7. Reflect on your overall situation, personally and professionally. Review the long-term goals you set for yourself six years ago, at the beginning of this epicycle. Have you progressed according to your plans in all sectors of your life? Have you overlooked anything important? Without being judgmental, measure your progress.

8. Keeping in mind that your current epicycle will be coming to an end in three years, that is, at the end of the 9 Personal Year, reflect on what you need to do to bring this cycle to a successful close. What projects need to be finished? What

relationships need to be released? Or healed? A review of your situation will teach you valuable lessons in goal setting, which you will be able to apply when the next epicycle begins. Overall, assess your progress. Did you set goals that were realistic and attainable? What would you do differently in the next cycle?

Exercise: Year-End Review

Complete this exercise at the end of your 7 Personal Year.

1. What benefits did you derive from your quiet times? In what ways have you grown?

2. How do you feel about your progress now? Are you content with your life?

3. What is the most important lesson you learned this year?

4. What new knowledge will you bring into your upcoming 8 Personal Year?

The 7 Personal Year Goal Setting and Planning Worksheet

As an aid to your yearly planning, complete the following worksheet. Set goals for each of your Key Life Sectors. In a 7 Personal Year, you are probably in need of some personal time out. Try to limit activities this year to those that are most important. You will not be inclined to the social life. Your goals should reflect your values and desires at this time of your life.

Goal Setting and Planning Worksheet My 7 Personal Year Reflection, Analysis, the Inner Life	
Key Life Sectors	*Goals for the year*
1	i
	ii
	iii
2	i
	ii
	iii
3	i
	ii
	iii
4	i
	ii
	iii
5	i
	ii
	iii
6	i
	ii
	iii

ELEVEN

Power, Accomplishment, Satisfaction

THE 8 PERSONAL YEAR

This is it! The big year, the peak of your epicycle. Of course, whether or not you've been working hard toward goals that reflect not only your talents and abilities but also your trends and cycles will determine if this will be a rewarding or a disappointing year. Composed of two 4s, the 8 is about as solid as it gets. The 8 represents the ultimate in material accomplishment.

The 8 is associated with the concept of karma, which is often perceived as a negative force. Karma simply reflects the law of cause and effect. Some people fear the 8, but shouldn't, especially if they have been sincere in their efforts. This is the year in which you will reap the fruits of your labors of the past seven years. If you have worked hard, were connected to your true life purpose, and applied the necessary efforts, then this year will bring success, accomplishment, and great satisfaction. If, on the other hand, you have lived your life without structure and purpose, floating along without direction, this year could be frustrating and discouraging, even filled with difficulty and additional stress. There really is no magic formula—hard work leads to results, the absence of work leads to failure and disappointment.

The 8 is the number of the paymaster, and it will reward you in direct proportion to the intention and effort you have expended. The 8 Personal Year is an excellent time to go all out and reach for your goals, to make them concrete. It is also an excellent time for business and financial activities. Now you can go for the position, the power, and the money. Financial rewards will equal the efforts you have made over the past several years. If, on the other hand, you have made unwise choices, the 8 Personal Year can spell financial disaster. Business failures and personal bankruptcies are not uncommon in the 8 Year.

This is the year in which your hard work will be rewarded. Recognition, promotions, bonuses, rewards, and career advancement are favored in the 8 Year, but along with these often comes added responsibility. Your leadership skills could be put to good use as you express your vision. You can make things happen now. You have the power, the authority, the skills and ability, as well as the experience to see things through to completion. You are the expert, the master, and the authority in your field. If you have dreamed of improving your personal or professional life, now is the time to go for it. Take control of your life. Feel the power of accomplishment. You've worked hard for it. Enjoy it!

Not all people respond to success in the same way. Amanda is a high-level human resources executive in the male-dominated aerospace industry. Up until the age of 38, like most women in her position, she hadn't given much thought to having a child. Then, to her surprise, in a 5 Personal Year (a year of sudden and unexpected change) she became pregnant and gave birth to a son. While on maternity leave, a 6 Personal Year (family responsibilities, balance), she discovered the joys of motherhood. In the 7 Personal Year (analysis and introspection), she gave a great deal of thought to her situation, reevaluating what was really important in her life.

After much reflection, Amanda concluded that although she had a fabulous career with all the perks and power any woman could possibly want, motherhood also mattered. She had reached a point in her life where she didn't want to be devoting all of her time and energy to her career. Knowing that she wouldn't be able to negotiate the hours and working conditions she needed to spend more time with her son, she did the one thing she thought would get their attention. At the start of her 8 Personal Year (a year of harvest and reward) and at the peak of her career, a position that she originally began in a 1 Personal Year, she handed in her resignation.

Note that Amanda is highly qualified, experienced, and very hard working. With an abundance of 4 energy among her numbers, she is a highly valued, dedicated asset to her employer. To her surprise, her boss turned around and offered her carte blanche to design the job conditions that would best suit her needs, if only she would reconsider her decision to leave the company. This unexpected turn of events put her in the unique position of paving the way for the many other women who had postponed motherhood for fear of jeopardizing their careers. Together they could now work out a solution for the special needs of women and motherhood, a project that would have far-reaching effects in her corporate environment, essentially all 8 Personal Year matters.

This example doesn't suggest that everyone with a job-related grievance should quit his or her job and expect to be offered the ideal work solution on a silver platter. What it does show is that if you do the work, when the time is right, the rewards and the recognition and the opportunities are usually there.

For some, the 8 Personal Year is a time for reevaluating long-term career goals. If you made questionable choices at the beginning of the current epicycle and are not satisfied with your direction, you could be facing some important decisions now. The 8 is a year of reckoning. Many people make important career changes in the 8 Personal Year. However, if you should find yourself in this situation, keep in mind that you are at the end of a cycle, and will not begin the next epicycle for another two years. This means that you will probably not have a complete picture of your future direction until the new cycle kicks in.

If you plan on taking a completely new direction now, be aware that important adjustments are likely to be made once you begin your next epicycle. If you can, avoid making long-term commitments, such as signing leases that last longer than the time that remains in your current cycle. Leave the doors open for change and new opportunities.

The best approach in the 8 Personal Year is to complete what you have begun over the past few years. Try to derive some satisfaction from immediate results rather than setting out on a new long-term direction. Work with what you have. When all is said and done, remember to reward yourself for your achievements, whether great or small. If you've thought things through, made appropriate decisions, and acted on them, then you've completed the process and have done well. Your accomplishments will be added to the foundation of your next experiences.

The 8 Personal Year Month by Month

Note that the following descriptions for the Personal Months are to be used as guide-lines for determining possible scenarios. Use the keywords from chapter 1 to interpret potential trends that apply to your particular lifestyle. Each person is unique, and each has a unique relationship with the numbers. Also keep in mind that the Personal Month trends are secondary to the Personal Year trends, and should be considered along with your Life Path and Birth Date numbers as well as your current Personal Year number.

JANUARY (9 Personal Month): Closure, Endings, Release

This epicycle is soon coming to a close, and you are probably starting to feel a strong urge to bring projects to completion. This is a good month to get some projects out of the way, especially those that might prevent you from successfully achieving your goals this year. You had plenty of opportunity to give serious thought to your goals and direction last year; now you are in a better position to make choices that are in tune with your inner purpose. Relieve yourself of unnecessary clutter, in all aspects of your life, and focus on your goals. If you have done the work, this year has the potential for great accomplishment. Although you could be feeling some uncertainty, avoid dwelling on fears or insecurities. Negative thinking will only drag you down.

FEBRUARY (1 Personal Month): Renewal, Beginnings, Initiative

February marks the beginning of the final thrust toward achieving material and financial rewards in the current epicycle. Now is the time to step up to the plate and give it all you've got. Be bold, courageous, and assertive. Your ambitions may rise to an all-time high as you set out to conquer the world. This is the time to overcome your fears and to be decisive. Yet, in your enthusiasm to forge ahead with your plans, avoid being overly aggressive or selfish. Begin new activities. Focus on your unique talents and abilities. Be creative and take initiative. If you are unable to overcome feelings of uncertainty, be patient with yourself, and don't force the issue. Things will fall into place very soon. Focus on accomplishment.

MARCH (11/2 Personal Month): Nervous Tension, Cooperation

Progress appears to slow down a bit this month. You will need to wait for the input of others before moving forward. Decisions are not entirely up to you at this time. Your heightened sensitivity and nervous tension could lead you to make impulsive moves. Wait for a day when you feel more balanced before making important decisions. Try to establish an environment of peace and harmony, in all aspects of your life. It is important that you remain open to the ideas of others, and refrain from making snap judgments. Keep your feelings to yourself; go for a walk, let the emotional tide fall before approaching others on matters that present potential conflict. At work, you can inspire others to support you in your efforts.

APRIL (3 Personal Month): Opportunities, Joy, Recognition

April should be a great month in many ways, especially in terms of social, personal, and business interactions. You feel optimistic and lucky, and good things are coming your away. Welcome business opportunities present themselves. Your efforts and hard work are recognized. Colleagues and friends are eager and willing to participate in activities with you. Try to delegate or postpone boring tasks. You are more in the mood to party than to work. Be aware of a tendency to spend money on frivolous things. Since this is a 3 Personal Month in an 8 Personal Year of accomplishment, look for ways of bringing a little creativity into your projects. Enjoy social events. Organize a company barbecue. If you are looking for a good time to schedule your annual vacation, April would be a good month.

MAY (13/4 Personal Month): Work, Details, Dedication

It's time to get back to work! If you are well organized by nature, you won't have any trouble getting back into the swing of things. If you aren't so well disciplined, you could find it rough going this month. By now, you realize the importance of focus and hard work in the achievement of your goals, and that your time of reckoning is drawing near. Take care of details and address those challenging projects head-on. Avoid being overly rigid and inflexible; if something isn't working, go around it and take another approach. You won't get points for banging your head incessantly against the wall. Nor is this the time to slack off and give in to laziness. Lack of focus could cause you to fail to reach your goals. Your efforts will pay off later this year.

JUNE (14/5 Personal Month): Surprises, Change, Liberation

Take advantage of new opportunities to move closer to your goals. Since 8 is a power year, you may want to stretch yourself now, reach beyond your comfort zone, take some risks. Keep your agenda and your schedule loose this month; unexpected situations are likely to arise and force you to change your plans. This can be an exciting month, a great time to promote yourself and your business. You are ready for change and adventure, so take a weekend or a few days off and dare to do something different. Have some fun, but remember to stay focused on your objectives for the year. Avoid excesses in all things. Remain flexible and don't fuss over details. You'll only become impatient. Delegate the annoying aspects of your duties. You're not in the mood to be tied down right now.

JULY (6 Personal Month): Responsibility, Measure, Balance

This is also an excellent month for career and money matters. You have been able to show what you can do, and your efforts will not go unnoticed. Growing feelings of empowerment extend to your personal life. You feel better equipped to make the changes that will bring increased harmony at home. Although you are feeling on top of the world, this doesn't mean that you should allow yourself to be overbearing and pushy with those persons who are close to you. At this time it is important that you exercise moderation in all things. Intent on attaining your goals this year, you could grow resentful of demands made on you by someone close. Remind yourself of what is really important. Try to keep things in perspective. Schedule a quiet weekend getaway with your partner.

AUGUST (16/7 Personal Month): Reflection, Analysis, Introspection

It's time to take a serious look at your accomplishments to date. The epicycle is soon coming to a close, and you need to measure your progress. This is not a good month for a family vacation, nor is it the best time for social events. If anything, a few days in contemplation in a quiet retreat, or some time spent reading or walking in the woods would be more helpful. You are very focused on your work and can handle complex issues. Your brain is working overtime as you try to come up with effective ways to overcome obstacles. Avoid feelings of superiority and negative attitudes toward others. Also, avoid being overly critical of yourself if you come to the conclusion that you may not be attaining the goals you had set for yourself in the time frame you had planned. Simply readjust your goals to reflect your current reality.

SEPTEMBER (8 Personal Month): Power, Accomplishment, Career

This is a power month, in a power year—a great month for money and business. Warn your family that you will be focusing on career more than on family and domestic issues. Obviously, this isn't the month for a family vacation. Be confident, authoritative, and dynamic, but remember that not everyone is running on your super-high level of energy. Avoid bullying and impatience. Be reasonable in your expectations. If you are impractical and unrealistic, you could pay a heavy price for your lack of judgment. Do not overextend yourself financially. Be patient, and make the most of what you now have. Change is coming soon; there will be plenty of opportunity to reconsider your options at a later date.

OCTOBER (9 Personal Month): Endings, Completion, Release

Finally, you are reaching the moment of completion. Bring those long-standing projects to a close. Be sensitive to the responses of others as activities reach their end. You could be feeling more emotional than usual, reluctant to release the old, hesitant or uncertain about what will be coming next. A business relationship could end now as you prepare to move on to other challenges. You may experience a sense of loss. Express kindness, compassion, and understanding in your interactions with others. Try to focus on others, rather than on yourself; donate some of your time to a charitable organization or community activity. Be generous. Let others benefit from your experience. Share your rewards and accomplishments.

NOVEMBER (19/1 Personal Month): Renewal, Beginnings, Energy

You may be sensing the start of a new year just around the corner and are eager for accomplishments and results. Feeling dynamic and energetic, you are ready to tackle whatever comes your way. You will need to balance enthusiasm with sensitivity. Forceful behavior will not serve you well. Avoid being overly aggressive and inconsiderate. Your current epicycle is coming to a close next year, after which a brand new period of your life will begin. However, some housecleaning is probably required before you can be free to move forward. There is no need to make rash decisions. You are feeling the confidence that is a natural consequence of your accomplishments of the past few years. This is an excellent month for all business matters. You could be forming new ideas or plans for the future. Again, take your time. You have a year of closure coming up, a 9 Personal Year.

DECEMBER (11/2 Personal Month): Inner Growth, Intuition

As this year of accomplishment winds down to a close, you may feel the need to pause, and reflect. You are particularly sensitive and responsive now, aware of your progress and growth. Tune into your intuition for insights, guidance, and inspiration for the coming 9 Personal Year, a time of completion and endings. You may be feeling somewhat vulnerable, uncertain as to where the upcoming changes will lead you. This can be an emotional time. Your idealism and feelings of specialness could prevent you from seeing things as they are. As much as possible, try to remain practical. Others may not agree with your unique or unusual way of doing things. You may find it difficult to express your feelings. Look for creative outlets to release some of that pent-up emotional energy. Prepare to wind down, to release, and let go.

The 8 Personal Year Workshop

Complete this workshop at the beginning of the year.

1. Relative to your Life Path, Birth Day number, and personal experience of the number 8, how do you feel about your personal accomplishments to date? Are you confident that you will be able to reach the goals you established for yourself seven years ago? If not, why not?

2. Recall the last time you experienced an 8 Personal Year. What was going on in your career and in your personal life at the time? Were you in a position of personal and professional fulfillment? If not, why not?

3. Relative to where you are in your life at this time, what do you feel you need to do to bring the current cycle to a successful close? Can you revise your goals so that you will reach a satisfactory level of accomplishment this year and next? It is far better to set realistic goals that you can reach than unrealistic goals that you will fail to meet.

4. Review your Key Life Sectors list. Are all these sectors still relevant at this time? Focus on power and accomplishment. Make any necessary changes or adjustments to your areas of focus. Express yourself with confidence.

5. Consider the long-term goals you set for yourself many years ago, both personally and professionally. Do you wish to keep these same goals for the next cycle? Is there something else you feel you need to accomplish in your life?

6. If you are self-employed, or in a position that normally does not lend itself to recognition, and have reached your goals, reward yourself for your efforts. Celebrate your achievements. Invite all your friends and have a big party.

Exercise: Year-End Review

Complete this exercise at the end of your 8 Personal Year.

1. In what areas did you accomplish your goals?

2. How do you feel about your progress now?

3. What is the most important lesson you learned this year?

4. What new knowledge will you bring into your upcoming 9 Personal Year, a year of completion and endings?

The 8 Personal Year Goal Setting and Planning Worksheet

As an aid to your yearly planning, complete the following worksheet. Based on your personal values, as well as on where you are now in your personal cycles, set goals for each of your Key Life Sectors. In an 8 Personal Year, you should be focusing on reaching full accomplishment of your goals. Consider dropping activities that may hinder this achievement. Your goals should reflect your values and desires at this time of your life.

Goal Setting and Planning Worksheet My 8 Personal Year Power, Accomplishment, Satisfaction	
Key Life Sectors	*Goals for the year*
1	i
	ii
	iii
2	i
	ii
	iii
3	i
	ii
	iii
4	i
	ii
	iii
5	i
	ii
	iii
6	i
	ii
	iii

TWELVE

Completion, Endings, Release

THE 9 PERSONAL YEAR

*

The 9 Personal Year wraps up the epicycle. It is a very important year in that it is the start of a major transition period and requires special attention and planning on your part. It is the end of a long cycle as well as a bridge to the next. It is a time of completion, a period of taking stock and winding down. As the current epicycle comes to a close, you will want to stand back, look at the big picture, consider where you have been and what you have accomplished, and begin to consider where you would like to go next. It is a time for releasing and healing any outstanding bumps and bruises you may have sustained on your journey to date. It is a period of integration; the time to absorb the lessons and experiences you have acquired.

It is not uncommon to experience nervousness, some anxiety, and heightened emotions, or even a sense of disorientation or confusion in a 9 Personal Year. An unknown future lies just around the corner, not yet fully determined, while the past still weighs down on you. This is a time for having a universal outlook on life, for opening your mind to broader horizons. Many people experience an explosion of creativity in a 9 Personal Year, giving them lots of ideas for possible future projects. It is very easy to become completely distracted now, as possibilities seem to jump out at every turn.

The 9 Year is a time for selflessness. The more you think of yourself, the more you are likely to grow confused or discouraged. Turn your focus toward others for a little while. Share your talents; volunteer with your favorite organization or a local community group. You have learned much in this epicycle. Internalize and integrate what you have received by giving it away.

This is the best time to clean house, both literally and metaphorically. De-clutter your life. Finish off or consider abandoning long-standing projects. Unload all unwanted or unnecessary clutter from your life, including people. In a word, get rid of all that might hold you back and weigh you down before moving forward. This is the best time to hold the garage sale of the decade!

What is no longer appropriate or needed now will likely work its way out of your life as new opportunities arrive on the horizon. The degree and nature of the housecleaning required in your 9 Personal Year will depend on where you are on your life journey. If you find that you have veered significantly off course, then this would be the time to consider releasing your hold of the reins of your wayward chariot. This may require that you quit an unhealthy work environment, leave a bad relationship, partnership, or marriage, or even leave town.

On the other hand, if your life is relatively on track, and you are heading in a healthy direction on your Life Path, then perhaps only moderate or light housekeeping is required, like getting to that garage you've been promising to clean out for what seems like forever. All forms of release will be beneficial, as it is an indicator to the unconscious mind that you are ready to let go of the old and prepare for the new. Keep in mind that a full glass cannot be refilled until it has first been emptied.

If you fear letting go, you may find this period challenging. In the 9 Year, there is a definite sense of something new about to emerge. However, you are still in the old epicycle, the new cycle not yet having been clearly defined. You may be uncertain about your future direction, which may only come into focus later in the year, or early in the next, the 1 Personal Year, when you experience a rebirth of energy and vision.

The 9 Personal Year is like the garden in winter, flattened and hidden beneath the snow, dormant, not visible. Not until spring do the grass and the flowers rise up again and come to life. Our experience of this transition from one cycle to the next is similar, with our vision and energy diminishing somewhat in the 9 Year only to be reborn in the 1 Personal Year when, rejuvenated and renewed, we see clearly once again the path that lies before us.

It is important to be patient in the 9 Year, to get plenty of rest, take care of yourself, and even visit your acupuncturist, naturopath, or other favorite health care professional. Since energy levels tend to diminish during this year, there appears to be a greater incidence of illness and health issues, especially for people over the age of 40. In northern latitudes where winters are harsh and flu viruses abound, the 9 Personal Year can prove to be challenging to the immune system, especially in the fall and early winter months.

In an ideal world, everyone would be allowed to take a year off at the end of the 9-Year Epicycle. Since we don't live in an ideal world, we need to create a lifestyle that favors our own health and well-being. If you are not in a position to take a sabbatical from your work, you may consider negotiating a four-day or three-day workweek or, if that isn't possible, try an extra-long vacation, especially during the second half of the year. This year, plan for some time off, rest, meditate, study, and travel. With a little planning—okay, with some efficient long-term financial planning—you can squirrel away enough money for an extended vacation in your next 9 Personal Year.

Many people suffer burnouts or illness in a 9 Personal Year because they refuse to slow down. Face it, the pace of life hasn't gotten any slower in the past thirty years, and since we've seemingly adjusted to this speeding up of life, it's not likely to slow down anytime soon. And if you want to stay in business, keep your job, hold your family together, and reach your goals, it's in your best interests to keep up the pace. Valiant efforts at keeping pace notwithstanding, eventually your mental, physical, or emotional body will suffer the brunt of this unnatural acceleration. That is why this point cannot be stressed enough: in a 9 Personal Year, slow down, downsize, unload, relax, and above all, get some rest. Schedule a spa day once a month (note that spas are open to men as well as women!), take up yoga, tai chi, go for massages, learn to meditate, breathe, go for quiet drives in the countryside, or take long walks in the park.

As this is a year of endings, keep in mind that anything begun in a 9 Year may not be carried through into your next year. For that reason, it is not wise to start important new projects, make major career moves, begin a business, or start a course of study until the next cycle begins. The 9 Year contains energy from an old cycle that is coming to a close. There is usually insufficient energy to sustain an important new endeavor for a long period of time. This also applies to relationships; many relationships begun in a 9 Year do not last very long.

Betty, a 4 Life Path with strong family values, was married in a 9 Personal Year and divorced twenty-seven years later, three complete epicycles later. Although the marriage lasted a long time, a *very* long time by today's standards, not long into the 1 Personal Year she realized that she had made a serious mistake. In those days, divorce was rarely an option and marriage was taken very seriously. Initially, Betty was determined to make it work. Then, children came. Following her 4 Life Path, she did what she had to do to ensure the wellness of her family. In the end, though, no amount of adjusting or bending could make her spend her entire life in an abusive relationship. Once relieved of her child-rearing duties and well established in a business of her own, in a 9 Personal Year, she finally left the marriage.

Sometimes, people will respond to this call for release by making strange choices. I have seen clients go off on radical tangents in a 9 Year, only to realize a couple of years later the error of their decision. Many of these wayward decisions are made under the mistaken assumption that anything new is better than the old. Tired of the old, people look for something new. However, given that the new cycle has not yet kicked in, it is best that you try cutting your hours, or exploring new opportunities on the side, before quitting your day job. Once the new year rolls around, you will have a better perspective on things and may even come to the conclusion that what you had wasn't so bad after all.

Carmen, a 9 Life Path with a 9 Birth Day, is a self-employed professional translator specialized in the field of ISO Standards. This is a very challenging job, which, over time, can lead to extreme mental fatigue. She had been operating a very successful business from her home for fifteen years when she reached her 9 Personal Year. She had lived in the Orient for a while, and had done some traveling over the years, experiences that she had very much enjoyed, which reflected the important number 9 influence.

At the peak of her epicycle, with a successful business supporting a comfortable lifestyle, she reached a point of saturation in her career. She was tired, and began to grow increasingly bored with the work, a new sentiment, since for most of the previous years, she had enjoyed the challenges of the technical fields she encountered in her profession. She needed a new interest. This is when her enjoyment of travel suddenly flourished into a new passion.

In the 8 Personal Year, ready to take on new challenges, she began a course of studies in the travel industry. In the following 9 Personal Year, eager to expand her horizons and by now very tired of her translation work, she jumped on an opportunity to work for a travel-related office. At first, she found it exciting to go to work outside the home. Learning new job skills gave her a well-needed renewal of energy. But the charm of the new adventure soon wore off; a desk job was definitely going to be boring. By the fall of that year, she concluded that over the years, her home-based translation business had afforded her a very good lifestyle, a level of freedom and autonomy she very much needed and enjoyed, and validation for being very successful in an intellectually and mentally challenging field, all the while allowing her to be present for her daughter while she was growing up. All in all, she concluded, she had a pretty good deal. In the following 1 Personal Year, Carmen renewed her commitment to her business. To fulfill her need for change, she engaged in major renovations in her home, updating the living spaces to better suit her needs and those of her college-age daughter.

At the end of his 9 Personal Year, Josh, an R&D tax consultant with degrees in economics and taxation decided to sign up for a three-year cabinet-making course. He had always wanted to know how to work with wood. Needless to say, once in his 1 Personal Year, his vision cleared up. He left this program and enrolled at university to further his education in a field that was more closely related to his R&D work. A minor distraction along the way, the cabinet-making course did give him the skills to build a deck in his backyard.

In a 9 Personal Year, focus on finishing off projects, get rid of clutter, and slow down. It's fine to open doors and explore new options; however, it's best not to make long-term commitments. Consider postponing the signing of leases or contracts until the new year. Try temporary approaches. If you are looking for a new line of work, take a part-time or temporary job in that field. Close the doors to what is outdated. Open doors on the new without making final decisions.

The 9 Personal Year Month by Month

Note that the following descriptions for the Personal Months are to be used as guidelines for determining possible scenarios. Use the keywords from chapter 1 to interpret potential trends that apply to your particular lifestyle. Each person is unique, and each has a unique relationship with the numbers. Also keep in mind that the Personal Month trends are secondary to the Personal Year trends, and should be considered along with your Life Path and Birth Date numbers as well as your current Personal Year number.

JANUARY (1 Personal Month): Autonomy, Self-Focus, Action

Now is the time to take the first steps in reviewing all aspects of your life, from personal to professional. Focus on yourself as you begin the last leg of your long, nine-year journey. Although you may experience growth and progress in your work this month, you could be starting to wonder if this is the direction you wish to pursue in the long run. This is the beginning of the end, and you may be feeling a little anxious to make changes in your life. However, the path you are to follow in the future has probably not yet made itself clear. Take action now, push forward with projects, and make some changes, as this is a 1 Personal Month, but be patient, insofar as the larger, long-term changes are concerned. It's not unusual to feel lost or confused now. You are beginning an important transition period.

FEBRUARY (11/2 Personal Month): Intuition, Inner Guidance

Projects could be moving at a slower pace right now. You may be questioning some of the decisions you made last month. Be receptive and, especially, be patient. Trying to change things too quickly will only result in frustration or confusion. Be alert to your heightened intuition. You are particularly sensitive to inspiration, and could be guided from within as to which steps to take in moving away from your old cycle and into your new one next year. Avoid being overly dramatic. It's not the end of the world, only the end of an epicycle. You feel particularly vulnerable and sensitive in personal relationships, and can take things personally. Try not to take yourself too seriously. Seek out the support of someone you trust, someone who doesn't have a special agenda for you.

MARCH (3 Personal Month): Sociability, Creativity, Optimism

You may enjoy social events this month or time spent with friends. Entertain and be entertained. You need a little fun time out, as the 9 Personal Year often proves to be emotionally draining. Complete activities or projects you started with friends. Use creative means to finish old projects. You are feeling more optimistic about the future, and can begin to think of your new life direction. However, this is not the time to act on ideas that might involve long-term decisions, no matter how exciting they may seem. This is a great month for a vacation. You feel more like relaxing than working. Even though a romantic encounter is possible, remember that this is a year of endings. Take your time. Wait until next year to make a serious commitment.

APRIL (13/4 Personal Month): *Work, Details, Order*

Work is your priority this month, so don't plan a vacation for April. You could experience frustration as you struggle with your daily tasks while seeking to release yourself from past and present limitations. This can be a confusing time. It is probably becoming clearer to you now that things are coming to an end, as they should in a 9 Personal Year. Keep in mind that endings make way for renewal and rebirth, which is what you will experience next year. Even though you are swamped with work, don't neglect your health. Fatigue could cause you to opt for fast foods or forgo regular exercise. Remain flexible as you work hard to bring projects to a close. Your dedication and persistence will bring progress in work, or home and garden projects.

MAY (14/5 Personal Month): *Instability, Change, Impatience*

You could be frustrated as you are pulled between a need to finish old projects and a desire to move forward. You are feeling a growing desire for change and for freedom, yet you still do not have a clear picture of your future path. Take things slowly. Consider new options as they present themselves, without making any long-term commitments. This is a time of deep inner change and transformation. Try something new, but don't throw out the baby with the bath water. Your options will become clearer as the year comes to a close and you move into your new cycle. Avoid impulsive, irresponsible decisions. Learn from past experience.

JUNE (6 Personal Month): *Responsibility, Balance, Healing*

This month brings a little more calm and peace into your life. You enjoy time spent at home, with family. This is a good month for a family vacation. Sort out your feelings, especially with regard to personal relationships. Are there issues that need to be looked at, old patterns released? Are your responsibilities toward others still valid now? This is a time for giving and for healing. Get some counseling. Although you may be feeling a bit lost, take the time to share your recent experiences with loved ones. They will appreciate the confidence you place in them during your time of confusion. Next month you will want to spend some time alone. Make sure your partner is comfortable with your need for solitude.

JULY (16/7 Personal Month): *Reflection, Solitude, Analysis*

You may feel the need to take a few days off by yourself this month, spend some time considering all those questions that have been simmering and bubbling to the surface lately. Although you may have some material or money concerns, you are not likely to find satisfactory solutions for those matters right away. Consider the ending of the current epicycle, the goals you had set for yourself, and your actual accomplishments. Steer clear of a tendency to be self-critical, negative, or gloomy. Release any selfish motives you may hold in your relationships. Look inward with the intention of learning and gaining a better understanding of yourself and others. Look for clues as to any changes you may have to make over the next several months to facilitate your transition into your next epicycle. Transition periods are generally not easy.

AUGUST (8 Personal Month): *Finances, Career, Accomplishment*

Business and career pick up momentum as projects move forward toward completion. You are feeling energetic and are focused on accomplishing your goals. Take a close look at finances and business matters; assess your income, debts, savings, and retirement portfolio. Concentrate on clearing out old debts and material obligations; avoid adding to your existing load. Remember that the more outdated baggage you can release now, the easier it will be to pursue a new direction in the upcoming new cycle. To ensure your success in a business matter, consider the situation from the perspective of the other person. Your dedication and diligence pay off and you could be richly rewarded for your efforts. Although you may be experiencing a high level of personal satisfaction, it is not yet time to make concrete decisions for the future.

SEPTEMBER (9 Personal Month): *Release, Completion, Endings*

A 9 Personal Month in a 9 Personal Year can generate considerable emotional turmoil. You know that change is inevitable, but the time of rebirth is not yet here. Finish off projects, clear up loose ends, rid your life of meaningless clutter. Invite some friends and have a gigantic garage sale! Be generous. Give of your time to a community organization. This month could mark the end of a long-standing relationship or job situation. Your emotions run high, and you feel more vulnerable than usual. This is a time of instability and uncertainty. Although you may be feeling anxious to move forward, avoid making long-term commitments now, whether in personal relationships or for career or business. Focus on release and completion.

OCTOBER (1 Personal Month): Renewal of Energy

October brings a much-needed renewal of energy after a long year of endings and uncertainty. You will be able to phase out the completion of old projects and begin considering your options for the next epicycle. This transition will occur gradually, over the next four to six months, so there is no need to jump ahead of yourself. You could be meeting new people now as you begin to explore possibilities. Be ready to replace old ways of doing things with new; old relationships with new; old ways of looking at life with a new outlook. Look within for guidance and follow your heart, but don't rush into a long-term commitment yet. Think it through first. Soon, there will be plenty of opportunities for decision making.

NOVEMBER (2 Personal Month): Pause and Reflection

Take time out to reflect on your new direction, leaving any unanswered questions for the time being. Wait for feedback, be receptive, and especially, be flexible. You can't do it all in one day. Your 9 Personal Year hasn't quite come to an end yet. Progress may appear slow now. Spend quality time with a close friend; nurture your valued relationships. Seek the counsel of a trusted mentor on those matters that trouble you most. A budding new relationship could be growing deeper this month. Give yourselves the time to get to know each other well before making any decisions. You are feeling vulnerable and emotional. Find some quiet time. Let the dust settle.

DECEMBER (3 Personal Month): Enjoyment, Relaxation, Friendship

The year and the epicycle are coming to a close, finally! You will be in the mood to celebrate and share good times with friends and family. Have fun, party, take a vacation, travel, and enjoy yourself. You've been through a grueling year! Your optimism level is on the rise as you sense the new cycle just around the corner. You are able to express yourself with flair and originality. Use your creativity freely. Good news is coming. Take your time with new projects; relax a bit. You've earned your time out. There is no need to rush into things. You will have plenty of opportunity to set plans in motion throughout the next year and into the next epicycle.

The 9 Personal Year Workshop

Complete this workshop at the beginning of the year.

1. Relative to your Life Path, Birth Day number, and your personal experience of the number 9, do you feel ready to bring your projects to a close this year? Have you made plans and provisions for taking extra time off? Have you scheduled an extended vacation? How will you get extra rest?

2. Go back to the last time you experienced a 9 Personal Year. Did you experience fatigue? Did you have health issues? Did you feel the satisfaction and relief of endings and release, or grief and sorrow at having to part with difficult situations?

3. Relative to where you are in your life at this time, what situations, activities, and relationships need to be ended now?

4. Review your Key Life Sectors list. There are probably some sectors that are no longer relevant now. Consider the probability that these will be modified or changed in the next epicycle. Prepare to release the old and make room for the new.

5. This year is really housecleaning time, in all ways. Make a list of unfinished projects. Prepare to discard baggage, feng shui your home—in fact, de-clutter all levels of your life, literally and metaphorically. Let go, release, and forgive.

6. Look for any outdated habits you may be holding on to. Explore all facets of your life: health, work, day-to-day activities, relationships. Ask yourself: Why am I holding on to these habits? What benefit do they serve in my life at this time? What would happen if I abandoned these behaviors now? How would my life be different? How would it be worse? How would it be better? What good habit(s) could I develop instead?

7. In what ways can you give back to your community? Plan on volunteering, sharing your talents and abilities with a local organization. Focus on helping others rather than yourself.

Exercise: Year-End Review

Complete this exercise at the end of your 9 Personal Year.

1. In what areas did you experience completion and release?

2. How do you feel about your accomplishments now?

3. What is the most important lesson you learned this year?

4. What new knowledge will you bring into your upcoming 1 Personal Year, a year of new beginnings?

The 9 Personal Year Goal Setting and Planning Worksheet

As an aid to your yearly planning, complete the following worksheet. Set goals for each of your Key Life Sectors. In a 9 Personal Year, you should be focusing on completion and release. This is a year of endings, and holding on to old baggage will only slow down your progress as you move into a new epicycle, and possibly a new Pinnacle next year. Avoid beginning new long-term projects. Your goals should reflect your values and desires at this time of your life.

Goal Setting and Planning Worksheet My 9 Personal Year Completion, Endings, Release	
Key Life Sectors	*Goals for the year*
1	i
	ii
	iii
2	i
	ii
	iii
3	i
	ii
	iii
4	i
	ii
	iii
5	i
	ii
	iii
6	i
	ii
	iii

THIRTEEN
✦ ✦ ✦

The Long-Term Cycles

If you're one of those people who consider themselves to be numerically challenged and you've gotten this far in the book, you're probably starting to really enjoy numbers by now. In astrological symbolism, mathematics is associated with the cardinal signs (Aries and Libra)[3] and in particular with the planet Saturn. Saturn, interestingly, is also associated with authority figures and, in particular, the father. I have noticed that many of the people who have trouble with numbers also have experienced negative relationships with their father or with an authority figure. Oftentimes the father was loving and caring, but he was simply absent.

I developed an early love of numbers and mathematics because it was the easiest way to establish common ground with my dad, a brilliant engineer. The infinite patience of his 9 Life Path tamed the restlessness and anxiety of my 14/5 Life Path. Throughout the difficult years of high school, no other subject had the appeal of algebra and geometry. Math was straightforward, clean, and direct, but mostly it was refreshingly logical. There was never any ambiguity with numbers, as there was with ideas, communications, relationships, and the shifting values of the sixties. With math, there was always one answer, the right answer, even if it was a zero. Opinions, feelings, preferences, or impressions didn't matter.

---

3. Pauline Edward, *Astrological Crosses in Relationships* (St. Paul: Llewellyn, 2002), 131.

Math was like solving puzzles. I'd stay up late at night just to attempt the level 3 problems, the advanced problems that were designed to really challenge our knowledge. If I couldn't get an answer, I'd go to sleep and, almost without fail, my brain would work out the answer during the night. I'd wake up the next morning and complete the equation. It was rewarding and validating. Here was something I could do right. Where everything else seemed confusing and often frightening, numbers never failed to come through. Mathematics was an oasis of order and logic in a world of chaos and uncertainty.

Another thing about numbers is that they don't lie. If your bathroom scale says that you weigh 185 pounds, there aren't many ways of interpreting your weight. If your bank account says that you're overdrawn by $6,000, well, there aren't too many poetic ways of expressing that you're in the red. If you're in a 4 Personal Year, there's no getting around it, you'll have to face work, family, and home responsibilities. If you're in a 9 Personal Year, you'll have to let things go.

Being familiar with the 9-Year Epicycle now, you are probably beginning to experience a greater sense of order and direction. So far, we've been working with short- and mid-term cycles: Personal Days, Months, and Years. In this chapter, we'll introduce a few more simple calculations, those concerned with the long-term cycles: the Pinnacle and Challenge numbers and the Life Path Periods. Although of less significant influence than the Life Path and Personal Year numbers, they do further refine the portrait of your life journey, adding valuable information for long-term planning and goal setting. With the addition of these cycles, you'll be able to put together a complete personal road map.

The Pinnacle Numbers

The Pinnacle numbers describe four periods along the journey, each with its own unique lessons and opportunities. Pinnacles provide you with opportunities that your Life Path number may not offer you. For example, if you are a 4 Life Path, you may become entrenched in habits and old ways of doing things. A 5 Pinnacle will force you to be innovative and to break up the routine.

Pinnacle changes often indicate a change of climate in your life, bringing a new set of experiences, challenges, and opportunities. Look to Pinnacle changes to help you understand why you are attracted to certain types of experiences. Pinnacle numbers will also describe the nature of the situations you are likely to encounter during a certain period.

When setting long-term goals, consider the climate indicated by your current and upcoming Pinnacles. If you are about to begin a 6 Pinnacle, for example, you can expect increased responsibilities both at home and at work. Given that the trend is toward service to others, this would not be a good time to go off on your own and do your own thing. Look to Pinnacle changes for important information about changing tides and new opportunities.

The First Pinnacle covers the vital formative years of the life and should be studied closely when raising children, or when considering your own motivations and early conditioning. It is found by adding the numbers of the month and day of birth, and reducing to a single digit. The Second Pinnacle number is arrived at by adding the day and year of birth, and reducing to a single digit. The Third Pinnacle is equal to the sum of the First and Second Pinnacle numbers while the Fourth Pinnacle is determined by adding the numbers for the Month and Year of birth. Each should be reduced to a single digit.

Pinnacle 1	Month + Day
Pinnacle 2	Day + Year
Pinnacle 3	Pinnacle 1 + Pinnacle 2
Pinnacle 4	Month + Year

Example calculations for a person born on June 29, 1971.

- Reduce the Birth Month number to a single digit or Master number: June = 6.

- Reduce the Birth Day number to a single digit or Master number: $29 = 2 + 9 = 11$.

- Reduce the year of birth number to a single digit or Master number: $1971 = 1 + 9 + 7 + 1 = 18$, reduce further, $1 + 8 = 9$.

- First Pinnacle number: Month plus Day, $6 + 11 = 17$, reduce to a single digit, $1 + 7 = 8$.

- Second Pinnacle number: Day plus Year, $11 + 9 = 20$, reduce to a single digit, $2 + 0 = 2$.

- Third Pinnacle number: First Pinnacle number plus Second Pinnacle number, $8 + 2 = 10$, reduce to a single digit, $1 + 0 = 1$.

- Fourth Pinnacle number: Month plus Year, $6 + 9 = 15$, reduce to a single digit, $1 + 5 = 6$.

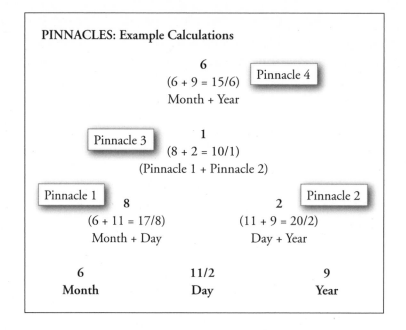

PINNACLES: Example Calculations

Pinnacle 4

6
(6 + 9 = 15/6)
Month + Year

Pinnacle 3

1
(8 + 2 = 10/1)
(Pinnacle 1 + Pinnacle 2)

Pinnacle 1

8
(6 + 11 = 17/8)
Month + Day

Pinnacle 2

2
(11 + 9 = 20/2)
Day + Year

6	11/2	9
Month	**Day**	**Year**

To calculate the duration of the First Pinnacle, subtract the Life Path number from 36. For example, if you have a Life Path of 8, your First Pinnacle would last from birth until the age of 28 (36 − 8). The Second Pinnacle would begin the year in which you turned 29. If your Life Path is 1, your First Pinnacle will last 35 (36 − 1) years and your Second Pinnacle will begin the year you turn 36. Pinnacles begin in January of a 1 Personal Year.

Duration of Pinnacles	
Pinnacle 1	36 – Life Path
Pinnacle 2	9 Years
Pinnacle 3	9 Years
Pinnacle 4	To end of life

The First Pinnacle can reflect limitations as well as opportunities, depending on your natural inclinations as indicated by the Life Path and Birth Day numbers. For a 5 Life Path person, for example, the discipline and order required during a 4 First Pinnacle can be challenging. Feelings of limitation and frustration may be even more strongly felt if the First Pinnacle is a 13/4 or if the Life Path is a 14/5. At the heart of the 5 Life Path is a deep desire for freedom. Although this person may resent the apparent limitations and rigor of the 4 Pinnacle, given a healthy and supportive environment, he may learn to work hard and perhaps develop the discipline and respect for order and perseverance that the 5 Life Path alone would not have offered.

The Second and Third Pinnacles, lasting nine years each, cover a large part of the middle life period. They reflect the climate of the productive years. An 8 in these periods is often very productive, offering significant opportunities for career advancement and financial growth. A 2 Pinnacle reflects a period of intense relationship issues, whether personal or professional, and is often a time for love and marriage, while a 6 Pinnacle can bring rewarding relationships, family life, and opportunities to develop and use management skills.

The Fourth Pinnacle, beginning after the Third Pinnacle and lasting for the remainder of one's life, reflects the nature of the latter phase of life, including the retirement years. For many, this is an important period of integration. Some people will question the significance of their lives now, looking for the value of their contribution to family, friends, or community. They reevaluate their career or job. Many people make significant adjustments at this time, seeking to better reflect changed values and learning experiences. Freed of the responsibility of raising a family and building a career, it's not unusual for people to embrace this period as a time of profound inner change and growth. On approaching their Fourth Pinnacles, many of my clients have expressed interests that are quite different from their lifelong day jobs, for example, transitioning from computer programming to photography, or from graphics to community politics.

Look to this Pinnacle when setting long-term goals. If you have a 4 Fourth Pinnacle, you may want to make sure that you have a hobby to fall back on when you retire. With 4 energy, you'll want to keep busy, work from home, or even renovate your home. If you have a 5 or a 9 Fourth Pinnacle, you may want to travel, explore the world, or express your creativity. A 7 Fourth Pinnacle will be indicative of a more reflective, quiet time of life, while a number 3 Fourth Pinnacle will likely offer plenty of opportunities to enjoy the social life or to express yourself creatively.

Also note any Karmic Debt influences behind the Pinnacle numbers. These can add an element of challenge to the period. A 19/1 Pinnacle might show a tendency to be overly willful, too centered on the self. This can result in conflict when dealing with others. A 13/4 Pinnacle may be experienced as being overly restrictive. A 14/5 Pinnacle can bring much instability and change. A 16/7 may indicate trouble in relationships or difficulty fitting in with corporate or other environments. As in all cases where Karmic Debt numbers are found, the degree of difficulty will be greatly attenuated and eventually transmuted to the positive expression of the number, as the individual, through continued growth and self-awareness, corrects the corresponding negative behaviors or attitudes.

Duration of the Pinnacles				
Life Path number	First Pinnacle	Second Pinnacle	Third Pinnacle	Fourth Pinnacle
1	0–35	36–44	45–53	54 →
2/11	0–34	35–43	44–52	53 →
3	0–33	34–42	43–51	52 →
4/22	0–32	33–41	42–50	51 →
5	0–31	32–40	41–49	50 →
6	0–30	31–39	40–48	49 →
7	0–29	30–38	39–47	48 →
8	0–28	29–37	38–46	47 →
9	0–27	28–36	37–45	46 →

When evaluating an upcoming Pinnacle, first consider your experience with the numbers. (See the exercise "My Experience of the Numbers," chapter 1.) If, for example, you generally lack courage, energy, and initiative, and are often fearful and dependant on others, you could be lacking in 1 energy. During a 1 Pinnacle you are likely to encounter situations that will challenge you to develop and use the positive traits of the 1, such as confidence, originality, and self-reliance. A 5 Pinnacle will bring opportunities for change, freedom, and new experiences, and will require flexibility and open-mindedness on your part. You can prepare for an upcoming Pinnacle change by becoming familiar with the energies of its corresponding number.

1 Pinnacle

This is a great time to express independence, courage, initiative, energy, determination, boldness, and enterprise. Focus on your personal goals, interests, and talents. It can be a period of rather intense self-discovery and should be used to develop your unique talents and abilities. You may find that you are pretty much on your own, and must proceed with little support from others. You will need to rely on yourself. Depending on your degree of self-confidence, this period can either be very productive or very difficult. If you are insecure and in need of support from others, you could find the 1 Pinnacle rather challenging, especially if circumstances push you to function independently. You have the chance now to forge new ground, to develop new approaches in your field of expertise, or to branch out on your own. Use your leadership, originality, creativity, and organizational skills.

2 Pinnacle

Relationships are usually very important during a 2 Pinnacle, and marriages are frequent at this time. This is not the time to think of yourself. Your sensitivity to the influences and needs of others is heightened, especially if this is an 11/2 Pinnacle. Your sensitivity could also extend to nature and the arts. You need a peaceful and quiet environment. You could be attracted to a helping profession such as counseling, a health-related field, or teaching. People are drawn to your charm, magnetism, and kindness. If you are a self-motivated and very independent person, you could find this period challenging, as you will be required to pay attention to the needs and demands of others. In a 2 Pinnacle, usually you are not alone. You may need to make adjustments to your lifestyle as you bring a spouse, partner, or children into your life. If you are in a troubled relationship, you could be faced with a divorce. Counseling, coaching, or mentoring could be very beneficial at this time. This Pinnacle requires that you be trustworthy, gracious, receptive, tolerant, diplomatic, considerate, and cooperative.

3 Pinnacle

The 3 Pinnacle can be a fun and enjoyable period. You will encounter plenty of opportunities for socializing, romance, and having a good time. In all areas, you should be positive and optimistic. If you feel yourself falling into negativity and moodiness, get help. The 3 can bring luck and fortunate opportunities and encounters. Tremendous creativity and imagination may be unleashed, and if you are an artist, you could get the lucky break that launches your career. This is an excellent time to expand your social network. There is often a strong need for self-expression, either verbally or through an artistic medium. Emotions can run high as sensitivity is heightened. It is easy to become scattered, distracted, and disorganized in a 3 Pinnacle. You will need to remain focused so as not to lose track of your long-term goals.

4 Pinnacle

A 4 Pinnacle usually requires that you tend to business, job, and family issues. It is a period of slow growth that requires persistence, consistent efforts, dedication, and perseverance. In some ways, it can be quite challenging. Limitations of time, money, and opportunity may be experienced. If a 13/4 Pinnacle, you could feel particularly frustrated. Courage and a positive attitude will need to be consciously maintained. You must focus on details and essentials. Order, organization, and method are required. Be patient and, especially, be realistic with your goals and expectations. Avoid becoming overly rigid. Home and property renovations or purchases are likely. Prepare for the future. Build a solid foundation now. Family obligations can hold you back. This can be a very productive time, especially if you are building a business or career. A 22/4 Pinnacle is demanding, but can lead to remarkable progress and financial rewards, especially if you are willing to work hard to build something of significance.

5 Pinnacle

A 5 Pinnacle can bring much movement, change, and varied experiences. It favors the public life. This is an excellent period for promoting yourself and your business. There may be little in the way of stability in a 5 Pinnacle. When experienced early in life, this usually indicates some uncertainty and many changes in the family environment. A broad education can be helpful. There is a tendency during a 5 Pinnacle, especially a 14/5 Pinnacle, to make impulsive or risky decisions. If, in your previous Pinnacle, you felt burdened by limitations and responsibilities, you may want to break free now. Beware of a tendency for exaggeration, unrealistic expectations, impatience, and irresponsibility. Remember to take the time to learn from past mistakes. The 5 usually calls for some degree of freedom and independence, so this would not be the best time to tie yourself down either personally or professionally. New experiences and travel are possible. This is an excellent time to express creativity and innovation in your work or business.

6 Pinnacle

A 6 Pinnacle is often a time where love and family life become important. Many people settle down and try to establish some level of balance in their lives in a 6 Pinnacle. You may want to bring some romance back into your relationship or spend more time with children and friends. This is a time for affection, harmony, and service to others. Unresolved relationship issues can come to a head. This can be a time of healing. If you have many 6s among your core numbers and have not yet established healthy boundaries between yourself and others, you could be doing far more than is necessary for others. You must learn that you don't need to sacrifice yourself in order to be loved or appreciated. If you are lacking in 6 energy, you could become resentful of the demands made by others on your time and energy. Accepting responsibility and service to others will bring many rewards. You could enjoy working as a volunteer in a community or charitable organization. This may be a good period to develop an artistic talent. This is also an excellent time to use your management skills.

7 Pinnacle

During a 7 Pinnacle, and especially if it is a 16/7, you could feel a bit at odds with the general trends in the world around you. There is a sense of differentness, a square peg trying to fit into round holes. This is a time of inner questioning, search, and spiritual exploration. This can be a challenging period for personal relationships as your focus is mostly inward. Keep the lines of communication with loved ones open. It is an excellent time for study, research, intellectual occupations, writing, solitary activity, meditation, and the inner life. It is important to guard against excessive feelings of specialness and even antisocial behavior. Enjoy doing things alone, but avoid hiding in solitude. This is not likely to be the most sociable or outgoing period of your life. Instead, socialize with people who have similar interests to yours. Material accomplishment and money take a back seat. In fact, you may be inclined to flee the material world. Specialize; hone your skills and develop an expertise or niche market for your business.

8 Pinnacle

The 8 Pinnacle very often is a period during which significant progress is made in business and financial matters. Success, money, rewards, and recognition are possible. Whatever your field of activity, you will have a pragmatic rather than emotional approach. You have vision, ambition, and the discipline and focus to achieve your goals. Reach for tangible goals and results. This is a power period. It is an excellent time for developing business, organizational, and management skills. You develop a taste for money and material rewards. Guard against putting career before family, or money before people. Becoming overly materialistic or insensitive could cost you important relationships. Maintain a sense of balance, be realistic, and clarify your objectives. Even if your goals are more lofty than materialistic, hard work, confidence, and diligence will lead to the rewards you seek.

9 Pinnacle

During a 9 Pinnacle, attention should be channeled away from personal interests, outward toward others, the community, or the welfare of humanity. When experienced as a First Pinnacle, a broad education should be considered. This is likely to be a time where you will be required to focus on the big picture, where a global approach rather than a personal or subjective approach will be most beneficial and productive. Compassion, open-mindedness, and understanding are necessary ingredients. This can be a period of high drama, where emotions run high and situations are experienced with great intensity. A relationship, marriage, project, job, or other activity may come to an end, generating feelings of sadness or loss. Endings are necessary now as they allow you to move forward. Travel, education, and large-scale undertakings are possible. Progress and success in business, the arts, and public life are favored now.

The Challenge Numbers

The Challenge numbers indicate specific qualities or attributes that need to be learned and integrated during a given period. A Challenge is usually experienced as the negative expression of a number, at least until its lesson has been learned. Although of less significant influence than the Pinnacles, Challenge numbers can provide important keys to identifying and clearing blockages to success. If a Challenge number is also found among the core numbers—for example, the Life Path number or name numbers—its influence is likely to be much weaker.

Challenge numbers are arrived at by calculating the difference between the numbers of the Birth Date, opposite to the calculations for the Pinnacle numbers. The Third Challenge number, also known as the Master Challenge, is the most important. The Master Challenge will be felt throughout the course of life, or until its lessons have been learned. The effect of the Fourth Challenge is almost negligible, and many numerologists ignore it altogether.

Challenge 1	Difference between Month and Day
Challenge 2	Difference between Day and Year
Challenge 3	Difference between Challenges 1 and 2
Challenge 4	Difference between Month and Year

Continuing with our example, for a birth of June 29, 1971:

- First Challenge number: Difference between Month and Day, 6 − 2 = 4.

- Second Challenge number: Difference between Day and Year, 9 − 2 = 7.

- Third Challenge number or Master Challenge: Difference between First Challenge and Second Challenge numbers, 7 − 4 = 3.

- Fourth Challenge number: Difference between Month and Year, 9 − 6 = 3.

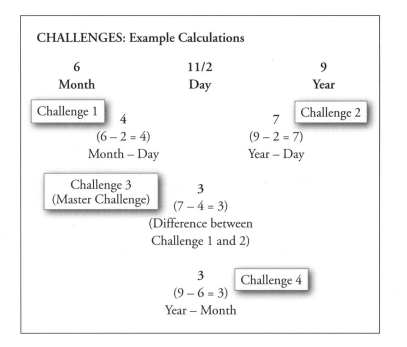

When calculating the Challenge numbers, reduce Master numbers before making the subtraction; use the single digit 2 instead of 11, and 4 rather than 22. Always subtract the smaller number from the larger. The Challenge number is the only place where a 0 result is possible. By the same token, there cannot be a 9 Challenge number.

The First Challenge covers the early, developmental years. If you have children, look to their first Challenge for clues as to their particular areas of difficulty. Helping them develop the positive traits of their Challenge number can contribute in an important way to the development of self-confidence and a positive self-image. Compare this number to the corresponding Pinnacle number. Following the example above, the 4 Pinnacle can signal an environment that favors work, discipline, and order, while a 3 Challenge number indicates shyness and an inability to express oneself.

The Challenges last as long as their corresponding Pinnacles, so that the First Challenge lasts 36 years minus the Life Path number, the Second and Third Challenges last 9 years each, and the Fourth lasts until the end of life.

Example Duration of Pinnacles and Challenges	
Pinnacle/Challenge 1	0–28
Pinnacle/Challenge 2	29–37
Pinnacle/Challenge 3	38–46
Pinnacle/Challenge 4	47–End of life

In our example, the business-minded, materialistic nature of the 8 Life Path will be reinforced by the 8 First Pinnacle, lasting from birth to the age of 28. This Pinnacle indicates an upbringing that favors material accomplishment, sometimes to the detriment of the values of the individual. The 3 Master Challenge could be experienced as a fear of self-expression, perhaps due to being subjected to excessive criticism during childhood, especially if unrealistically high standards of achievement were set by family and the environment during the formative years. The 4 Challenge, normally indicating a reluctance to conform to order, discipline, and structure, may not be experienced too harshly, as the natural drive and ambition of the 8s can motivate the person to work hard and focus on his goals. With a Life Path of 3 or 5, however, the person may have found those formative years to be rather limiting, provoking rebellious or reactionary tendencies.

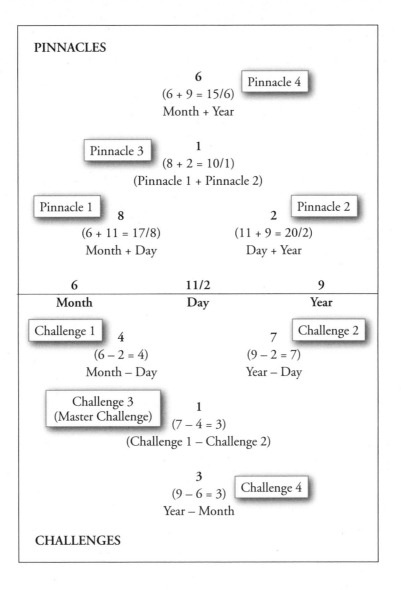

PINNACLES

6
(6 + 9 = 15/6)
Month + Year

Pinnacle 4

Pinnacle 3
1
(8 + 2 = 10/1)
(Pinnacle 1 + Pinnacle 2)

Pinnacle 1
8
(6 + 11 = 17/8)
Month + Day

2
(11 + 9 = 20/2)
Day + Year

Pinnacle 2

6	11/2	9
Month	**Day**	**Year**

Challenge 1
4
(6 − 2 = 4)
Month − Day

7
(9 − 2 = 7)
Year − Day

Challenge 2

Challenge 3
(Master Challenge)
1
(7 − 4 = 3)
(Challenge 1 − Challenge 2)

3
(9 − 6 = 3)
Year − Month

Challenge 4

CHALLENGES

1 Challenge

The principal lesson here is one of independence and self-reliance. Learn to trust your instincts and not give in to the stronger characters around you. You need to develop courage, initiative, autonomy, ambition, strength of purpose, and direction. Learn to stand up for yourself. Find passion in what you do, otherwise you may lack the energy to follow through on your projects. Learn to forge ahead without the support of others.

2 Challenge

You can be self-conscious, shy, timid, and lacking in self-confidence. You are overly sensitive and concerned about what others might think of you. Fearful of being judged, you prefer to remain a wallflower. You tend to make mountains out of molehills. You have difficulty relating to others in a balanced manner. The world does not revolve around you, nor will you disappear if you venture out into the world. You must develop patience, loyalty, diplomacy, tact, discretion, and the art of compromise.

3 Challenge

Your shyness and tendency toward self-criticism could prevent you from expressing yourself freely. Your innate creativity may be suppressed. Negative and critical influences in your environment cause you to be cautious and inhibited. You are too serious. You need to learn to have fun and relax, take things less seriously. Go out with friends. Being social doesn't necessarily mean being superficial.

4 Challenge

Your challenge is to learn to appreciate order, organization, dedication, and discipline. You dislike work and responsibility, or anything that appears to cramp your style. On the other hand, you may obsess over details and be overly rigid and narrow-minded. Stand back from the trees so you can see the forest. You need to develop a practical and realistic approach in all areas of your life.

5 Challenge

You need to tame your restless, impulsive, and impatient temperament. You seek change for its own sake, or you fear change and hold on to old ways of doing things. You need adventure, stimulation, and new experiences and may overindulge in food, drugs, or alcohol. If you don't want to see a trail of unfinished business behind you, learn to focus on your goals and finish what you start.

6 Challenge

You have high standards and are overly idealistic. In your mind, you wish to live in a world in which everything is perfect, just the way you want it. You are intolerant, demanding, and manipulative, and you like to have things done your way. You need to learn the rewards of being of service to others, to simply give freely, no strings attached. Would you rather be right or be happy? Learn to work with others.

7 Challenge

You experience a sort of divine discontentment, at odds with the world, seeking answers and never finding them. At times you feel superior, knowing it all. At other times, you feel lost, uncertain about anything. Deep fear keeps you from looking too far beneath the surface. You need to find a comfortable balance between your ability to reason and allowing yourself to have faith in something greater than you.

8 Challenge

Money, status, power, and material goals take up much of your time and energy. Fear of scarcity motivates your every action. You are overly materialistic, and you may disregard the needs of others to get what you want. You need to balance your priorities, learn the value of service to others. Seek goals that will benefit others. Discover the rewards of giving and sharing. No man is an island, no matter how wealthy.

0 Challenge

When a 0 Challenge number results, it should be given a broad interpretation, reflecting a life in which a wide range of possible learning situations can occur. You may have difficulty clearly defining your desires, and you can have a sense of uncertainty when expressing yourself or when attempting to manifest your inner being. You may have a more diffuse sense of self.

Exercise: Complete Your Pinnacles and Challenges Chart

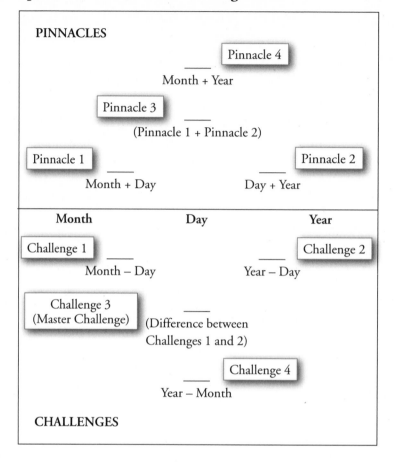

From the *Duration of Pinnacles and Challenges* table, complete the chart below for your Pinnacles and Challenges.

My Pinnacles and Challenges	
Pinnacle/Challenge 1	
Pinnacle/Challenge 2	
Pinnacle/Challenge 3	
Pinnacle/Challenge 4	

The Life Path Periods

In many cultures, the average life span is seen as being broken down into three broad periods: youth, adulthood, and maturity. These three periods correspond to the Life Path Periods in numerology and are also related to the Birth Date. Of less significant influence than the Pinnacles, they do provide a general backdrop to the events and situations encountered along your journey. The first Life Path Period is derived from the Birth Month; the second, or middle, period from the Birth Day; and the third and final Life Path Period from the Birth Year. In our example of a person born June 29, 1971, proceed as follows:

1. First Life Path Period: reduce the Birth Month to a single digit: June = 6.

2. Second Life Path Period: reduce the Birth Day to a single digit, the 29th, 2 + 9 = 11/2 (do not reduce the Master number 11).

3. Third Life Path Period: reduce the year of birth to a single digit, 1 + 9 + 7 + 1 = 18, 1 + 8 = 9.

6	11/2	9
Month	**Day**	**Year**
1st Life Path Period	2nd Life Path Period	3rd Life Path Period

In this case, the First Life Path Period is a 6, the Second is a 2 with an 11 influence, and the Third and final period is a 9. The 6 contributes an element of service and responsibility toward others, a need to be loved, while the 11/2 Birth Day number, in effect throughout all of life but more important during this period, will add sensitivity and a certain level of ingenuity in dealing with problems and issues, all the while softening the effect of the strong 8 influence discussed in the section on Challenge numbers. The 9 will give a sense of community, perhaps a desire to travel, expand horizons, and discover the world.

The Master numbers 11 and 22, as well as the Karmic Debt numbers, 13/4, 14/5, 16/7, and 19/1, are taken into consideration in the interpretation of the Life Path Periods. For example, throughout these years it might be difficult for a person with a 16/7 Life Path Period to find satisfaction in his personal or business relationships. He may struggle with the desire to fulfill his personal ambitions, regardless of his responsibilities toward others. Developing an awareness of the needs and concerns of others would be essential to his success and happiness during this Life Path Period.

The transition from one Life Path Period to the next is gradual and is generally felt as a mild trend change. Real change is usually experienced at the start of the epicycle, that is, in the 1 Personal Year following the Life Path Period change. For some, the transition from one period to another can be relatively smooth, a natural progression from one phase of life to the next, while for others, the transition can cause some tension or anxiety, as values and goals are reconsidered. The degree of difficulty or ease of a transition will be determined by the degree to which you have learned your lessons in previous periods as well as your ability to deal with the energy of the number of the period.

If you have read other numerology books, you may find a slight difference in the timing of the Life Path Periods. As they parallel the cycles of astrology determined by the progressing Moon and transiting Saturn, I allocate between twenty-seven and thirty years for each period. This way, they tie in more closely with the important turning points most people experience. Look to the start of a new epicycle, a 1 Personal Year, for the most significant turning points.

The lessons learned, the talents and aptitudes developed, and the challenges overcome during the first Life Path Period will determine in large part your success in subsequent periods. These are the important foundation years, the formative years where values are entrenched, where hopes and dreams are either nurtured and encouraged or suppressed, or, all too often, even shattered. Issues that have not been adequately dealt with at this time will surface later in life, particularly during high-stress periods.

Youth	Adulthood	Maturity
Development, learning, establishment of values, beliefs and patterns, self-reliance, confidence	Productivity, contribution, responsibility, construction, family and community	Integration, transformation, release, fulfillment, self-actualization, giving back, healing, universality

The end of the First Life Path Period and the start of the Second Period is marked by a number of important cycles in both astrology and numerology, including the first Saturn return, the first progressed Moon return, the First Pinnacle, and the end of a 9-Year Epicycle. For many people, it is a significant time of decision making and buckling down to the serious business of adult life. This is when people marry, or divorce, especially if they married young and for the wrong reasons. Many look for job security and consider having a family. There is a letting go of childhood and sometimes the abandonment of youthful ideals, hopes, and dreams. The Second Life Path Period relates to the productive phase of life, which is generally fast paced and filled with a broad range of activities as well as a high level of responsibility.

The Third Life Path Period, maturity, is regarded by some cultures as the age of wisdom. It is marked by the second Saturn return and the second progressed New Moon, and combines its energy with the Fourth Pinnacle number. The transition into this period is often a time of uncertainty and much inner growth and change. Men and women tend to experience this period differently. Men, who usually play the role of provider during the middle years, are often relieved of this burden by the time they reach maturity. Many will turn toward questions centering on the meaning of life, the inner life, or quality of life. This period can bring out unexpressed or repressed desires, talents, and abilities. It's not uncommon to find men in their late fifties and early sixties taking up hobbies that encourage self-expression such as painting or even cooking. Others will seek out ways of exploring the nurturing side of the human experience by looking for someone they can take care of.

On the other hand, women entering the Third Life Path Period have completed the nurturing phase of life. Relieved of the burden of child-raising and now sporting a brand-new set of hormones, these women are looking outward into the world, seeking avenues of manifestation, looking for ways of making a contribution to the world. There seems to be a turnstile at the kitchen door, with men going in and women going out.

The degree to which you have overcome obstacles, developed talents and abilities, and healed childhood wounds during the first two periods will determine the choices you will make as well as your ability to take advantage of the opportunities inherent in the trends of this Third Period. In recent years, with the aging of the large boomer generation, this phase of life has become very important. Rather than looking for ways of quietly disappearing into the sunset, many people in their fifties and sixties are playing catch-up with themselves, often trying to fix the broken pieces of the puzzle of their lives with the hope of experiencing a deeper and more rewarding final period.

The Life Path Periods describe undercurrents at work throughout the broad periods of the life, and should be interpreted according to your basic nature, age, circumstances, and life experience. Although of less importance than the Life Path and Pinnacles, they do add a general background tone. Note also that these periods should be considered in relationship to the broader picture indicated by the Life Path, Birth Day, and other numbers. Everyone born in March has a 3 First Life Path Period. This doesn't mean that all people born in that month experience a happy social and family life in that period.

1 Life Path Period

This is a period of much activity and intensity. Your focus is on developing originality, autonomy, and individuality. It's about you. This can be a challenging time, as it requires much self-reliance, offering little in the way of outside support. If you dig deep, build up your courage, and overcome any feelings of insecurity or inadequacy, excellent progress can be made, especially in a Second or Third Period. If a 19/1 Period, you must guard against selfishness, forcefulness, and egotism. If you have learned your lessons well, this period can push you to develop your abilities in a way that you might otherwise not have done. Great personal success and achievement are possible.

2 Life Path Period

In the 2 Life Path Period, your attention will be focused on personal and professional relationships. Progress is slower now, and in some ways depends on the input or contribution of others. You will probably need to make certain compromises. You feel things deeply and may not know how to channel all that emotional energy. You may seek to please in order to obtain the approval of others. You enjoy working with others and may find yourself in a helping profession. You understand the value of support, cooperation, and collaboration. You must learn to be patient, sensitive, and diplomatic, while not losing yourself in your relationships. If an 11/2 Period, you will be particularly sensitive, and have a sense of importance, as though you have a unique purpose or mission in life.

3 Life Path Period

This is a time for developing a healthy ability to express yourself. Develop communication skills; keep a daily journal of your thoughts and impressions. Latent artistic talents may surface now. This is an excellent period to pursue a career in writing, theatre, music, photography, drawing, or painting. You prefer fun and pleasure to work and discipline. You may be scattered, lacking in focus. If you wish to achieve your goals, you must develop perseverance and will probably need to sacrifice some of those fun activities. Avoid being wasteful of time and resources. This is a very social time, with many opportunities for developing your personal and professional network of contacts. This is an excellent period for building a business involving communications and entertainment, but you will need to get yourself organized, focused.

4 Life Path Period

The 4 Life Path Period is the time for home, family, and hard work. You plod along slowly, paying attention to details, dealing with all manner of duties and obligations. To get through this period, you will need to accept and perhaps even develop an appreciation for order, structure, and organization. If you are in a field of work that you enjoy, this can be a very productive period. If you remain practical and realistic in your expectations, you will be rewarded with solid, tangible results. Throughout this period, you may have to work hard to maintain a positive outlook. Avoid getting bogged down with details or becoming overly rigid in your work habits. Stand back once in a while and take a look at the broader picture. If a 13/4 Period, you may grow frustrated as work and other obligations limit and even restrict your freedom. If a 22/4 Period, you will be driven to build something of value to the community. Hard work and total dedication will be required of you now.

5 Life Path Period

This Life Path Period can bring much change, adventure, new experiences, and instability. You can expect surprises and unexpected turns of events. There is likely to be much movement, travel, and excitement. This is definitely not a stagnant period, and sometimes can bring much uncertainty. Many moves or job changes are possible. The need for freedom is a constant factor. This is a period of much growth and expansion. There is little that ties you down. Make sure your lifestyle is flexible, if not portable. If a 14/5, you may find it difficult to focus on one area of interest, drifting from one new opportunity to the next. You enjoy change and flee responsibility. You dislike being tied down. Constantly on the move, you fail to learn from experiences. This is not the most stable time for long-term relationships or projects. You will need to learn to finish what you start.

6 Life Path Period

Family, friends, and the support of close personal relationships become a priority during the 6 Life Path Period. You experience both the joys and the frustrations inherent in your responsibilities toward others. You appreciate the rewards of service to others, of giving and of receiving love. At other times, you may experience the problems encountered when caring for family and loved ones, especially the demands made on your time and resources. This is a time for love and marriage, but if relationship issues have not been dealt with, it is a time for divorce. You can experience outstanding career and business advancement if you work in harmony with others, respecting your obligations, and establishing healthy boundaries between yourself and others. Find the balance between respecting your commitments while avoiding becoming meddlesome and controlling.

7 Life Path Period

The 7 Life Path Period requires that you bring your attention inward, away from the hustle and bustle of the material world. Sometimes, there is a loss of interest in money and material things, at times even financial loss. This can be a quiet phase of life, with little inclination for the social life or for worldly pursuits. This is an excellent period for study, research, specialization, spirituality, and self-discovery. If a 16/7, you must guard against isolating yourself completely from the outside world. You could feel unusual or in some way special, even superior to others. This can be a challenging period for personal relationships as you find it difficult to share your thoughts and feelings. It is possible that you may have difficulty understanding what is going on inside yourself and are uncomfortable sharing this with others. You will have to make efforts to remain positive and to maintain your ties with the outside world.

8 Life Path Period

During an 8 Life Path Period, you learn the value of money and material success. This is an excellent period for career and business. There will be plenty of opportunities for developing and using your management, leadership, and organizational skills. You have vision and ambition and are likely to be very focused on achieving your goals. Scarcity and lack of money can push you to develop your abilities and overcome adversity. You have much energy and drive. Guard against putting material goals ahead of people. Family can very easily take a back seat to career in an 8 Period. You will need to make conscious efforts to nurture your personal relationships.

9 Life Path Period

The 9 Life Path Period tests your ability and willingness to focus on interests other than your own. This can be a period of much drama and heightened emotions. Nothing appears like a small matter now; everything seems to be important. You tend to make mountains out of molehills. The more you focus on your personal needs and interests, the less things seem to work in your favor. A universal outlook and approach is needed now. Focus on what is for the good of the community. Relationships or long-standing situations may come to an end. You may find it difficult to release the past and move forward. This can be an excellent period for an artistic or creative career, as well as for the public life. An attitude of love, acceptance, and tolerance will be most helpful now.

Exercise: Calculate Your Life Path Period Numbers

Life Path Periods		
Month	**Day**	**Year**
1st Life Path Period	2nd Life Path Period	3rd Life Path Period
0–28	29–57	58 onward

Insert your Life Path Period numbers in the table above the Day, Month, and Year. Note that you will find your three Life Path Periods on the Pinnacles and Challenges chart that you completed in the previous exercise, above Month, Day, and Year.

FOURTEEN

Putting It All Together

CHARTING THE 9-YEAR EPICYCLE

Now that you've acquired a real taste for numbers, we'll combine all the data from your Birth Date and complete your personal road map. When interpreting any of the numbers, always keep in mind the importance of putting the information into context. As we've already seen, age is a factor. What might appear to be challenging at one time of your life may be experienced as an opportunity at a later date. Also, your experience of the numbers is not static. You may express the energy of a number negatively in the early years, but with learning, growth, and improved self-awareness you will naturally progress to the positive expression of that same energy. Your experience of the numbers evolves as you grow, but by the same token, your understanding of the numbers will contribute to deeper self-knowledge. Learning about your numbers is a win-win situation!

> *Success is not the key to happiness. Happiness is the key to success. If you love what you are doing, you will be successful.*
>
> ALBERT SCHWEITZER

Most of us can look back over our lives and recall periods that were in some way remarkable. There are difficult and challenging times, and periods of insecurity, loss, fear, and confusion. Then there are those happy, joyful, safe, and prosperous times, and other, sometimes lengthy periods that are entirely insignificant and forgettable. At any given moment, several cycles may be operating simultaneously, and it is the study of these cycles that will enable you to identify a particular trend or climate. A helpful tool for short- and long-term planning is the 9-Year Epicycle table. Don't worry, this step doesn't involve any calculations. The Epicycle table consolidates your currently active numbers in an easy reference format.

As shown in chapter 1, the numbers 1 through 9 trace out a sort of organic flow in the life experience, with each number adding an essential component to the growth and development of the next and eventually to the whole. The cycle begins with an initial burst of energy and a sense of renewal in the 1 Personal Year, builds to a peak in the 8 Personal Year of accomplishment, then winds down and fades out in the 9 Personal Year of completion and endings in preparation for the next 9-Year Epicycle. The more effectively you integrate the lessons of the numbers as encountered along the way, the more successful your experience of this and subsequent periods will be. For example, if you work hard at establishing healthy relationships in your 2 Personal Year, you are more likely to come across opportunities, or "lucky breaks," in your 3 Personal Year by knowing the right people in the right places.

Example 9-Year Epicycle, for a person born June 29, 1971										
Life Path					8					
		Pinnacle			2			∗		
	9	1	2	3	4	5	6	7	8	9	1
Year	1999	2000	2001	2002	2003	2004	2005	2006	2007	2008	2009
Age	28	29	30	31	32	33	34	35	36	37	38
		Challenge			7					
Life Path Period					11/2					

In our example for a person born June 29, 1971, combining the Personal Year numbers with the Pinnacles, Challenges, and Life Path Periods, we can now map out a complete 9-Year Epicycle. From the table, we can see that in 2006, this person is in a 7 Personal Year and is approaching the end of the current epicycle. As the cycle peaks in 2007, in the 8 Personal Year, then winds down in 2008, the 9 Personal Year, efforts would be best employed in bringing projects to completion. The 2 Pinnacle and 11/2 Life Path Period indicate that relationships play an important role throughout the period, while the 7 Challenge shows a need to look beneath the surface of situations and circumstances and perhaps an inability to deal with solitude. With an 8 Life Path, this person will generally seek to fulfill material goals above all else, but this particular period of life will have brought important opportunities for discovering the benefits of establishing fruitful relationships and for learning to be cooperative and sensitive to the needs of others—valuable traits for an 8 Life Path person with an executive management job.

Among the cycle changes, the Pinnacle changes are likely to signal the most significant turning points, and can be felt a few months before the actual change. Once the energy of the new Pinnacle has been engaged, the previous Pinnacle dissipates quickly. Don, the 13/4 Life Path IT company president who joined a group of bikers for a 2,500-mile trek to the East Coast in his 1 Personal Year (see chapter 4), had also just moved into his final Pinnacle, a number 5. He described his adventure as a need to get away, a desire for freedom, a typical experience for a 5 Pinnacle. Toward the end of that trip, Don experienced an additional challenge. His bike broke down and he had to stay behind on his own in a small town across the border for a couple of days until his bike was repaired. Although for many this would not seem to be an extraordinary feat, for Don, given his cautious 13/4 Life Path and 1 Master Challenge, this was an important exercise in stretching boundaries and developing courage and autonomy.

How you relate to a particular trend depends on a variety of factors. Not everyone responds in the same manner to the same situation. An avid skier will express great joy upon learning of a late-March forecast of fresh snow, while an ardent gardener might bemoan the delay indicated by the same forecast. A period of 4 energy favoring hard work, structure, and organization might be a welcome trend for a forty-something businessperson working to establish a solid plan for his new venture, while this same period might not be as welcome for the 16-year-old guided by raging hormones with nothing but partying on his mind. When judging upcoming trends, take your particular circumstances, including age, life experience, and degree of self-awareness, into consideration.

Numbers should always be interpreted in relationship to each other. Their meanings should be blended for a more accurate interpretation. When you combine your Life Path, Pinnacle, Challenge, and Life Path Period numbers, a more complete picture emerges. At the same time as she discovered painting, Linda (see chapter 6) also found love. She had just begun a 6 Pinnacle, a complementary energy to her 3 Life Path that favors not only artistic self-expression, but also love and romance. In the years leading up to the 6 Pinnacle, she had faced a 2 Challenge. During that period, also a 3 Life Path Period, she had spent considerable time and effort initially dealing with and eventually healing long-standing relationship issues.

Ivan, the 11/2 Life Path who was struggling to assume family and work responsibilities in his 6 Personal Year (see chapter 9) was also in a 6 Pinnacle. This doubling of the 6 energy intensified the need for responsible action, something he was not ready to assume. At the same time, he had a 2 Challenge, requiring that he think of others rather than of himself. This 2 Challenge was reinforced by the 2 Life Path Period. With a 1 Master Challenge, Ivan had yet to find the balance between his needs and those of the people for which he was responsible. Fixated on his own specialness, he was unsuccessful in all areas of his life. A period that might otherwise have been experienced as very favorable for family and career was experienced as challenging, stressful, and unfulfilling.

Louise, on the other hand, experienced similar numbers in an entirely different manner. A 6 Life Path with an 11/2 Birth Day and a 1 Master Challenge, she is a highly educated woman with a prominent position in the business community. As her numbers would indicate, she has excellent management and people skills, all of which have served her very well over the years. During her Second Life Path Period (11/2), she had developed an intense and richly rewarding relationship with a man who lived on the other side of the continent. This relationship was significant, as it had allowed Louise to connect with deeper aspects of herself, including the poetic and artistic, natural expressions of her 6 Life Path and 11/2 Birth Day. However, during that time, neither was in a position to abandon career or family obligations. As she approached her Third Life Path Period, a 6, she realized that she was ready for change. She accepted a marriage proposal from the love of her life (6 Life Path Period) and, upon starting a 9 Personal Year (endings and release), made preparations to leave her important position, move across the country, and start a completely new life.

Exercise: Complete Your 9-Year Epicycle Chart
Having completed all the calculations that relate to your Birth Date, you are now ready to put it all together and tell your own story. Complete the table below with your personal information:

- Life Path number (chapter 2)
- Personal Year number (chapter 3)

- Current Pinnacle, Challenge, and Life Path Period numbers (chapter 13)
- Calendar years and ages associated with your current epicycle

My Current Epicycle												
Life Path												
		Pinnacle							*			
	9	1	2	3	4	5	6	7	8	9	1	
Year												
Age												
		Challenge										
Life Path Period												

Tips for Interpreting Your Numbers

- When completing the Yearly Planning and Goal Setting worksheets, include your current Pinnacle, Challenge, and Life Path Period numbers for a more complete picture. The Life Path Periods act like background music, while the Pinnacles indicate a specific theme for the period.

- Note any influences that might cause tension. For example, if you have a 7 Life Path and are currently experiencing a 2 Pinnacle and 6 Personal Year, you may find yourself pulled between a desire to tend to your own business (7) and the needs of family and friends (2 and 6). If you are not attentive, your relationships could suffer.

  Periods of tension can offer some of the greatest opportunities for growth. They can be like the grain of sand that irritates the delicate lining of the oyster shell, causing it to secrete the nacre that will eventually turn the irritant into a pearl. Use these periods to develop new skills or round out abilities and personality traits.

- Note the presence of Karmic Debt and Master numbers in the Life Path, Pinnacles, and Life Path Periods. These will indicate more intense lessons and experiences.

Once their lessons have been learned, you can expect to manifest the greater potential of the number.

- Also note the repetition of numbers, for example a 6 Personal Year with a 6 Life Path and a 6 Pinnacle. The repetition of numbers can indicate a supercharged energy, making it difficult to manifest the number in a positive and balanced manner.

- Before making important decisions, consider your position in your current epicycle. Are you at the beginning, middle, or end of your epicycle? This will help you determine your course of action. Early in a cycle, you might undertake new long-term projects; in the middle, you will want to focus on productivity, while at the end of an epicycle, you would bring projects to completion. If, for example, you have been inspired in a 5 Personal Year to take a completely new direction, keep in mind that in 4 years you will be experiencing a transition period. Ask yourself whether you are simply in need of a little freedom and adventure, as is often common in a 5 Year, or if the change is truly justified. If there is a change of Pinnacle number in your next cycle, you will likely be experiencing change in your new venture.

  Swamped with work, typical of a 4 Personal Year, a client of mine missed his annual consultation. In the following 5 Personal Year, also in an 8 Pinnacle, he eagerly ventured out into real estate. Had he consulted, he would have learned that this was not a favorable time to make important financial investments, and he lost money.[4] The material ambition of the 8 combined with the risk-taking nature of the 5 should be approached with caution. Sometimes it can lead to substantial gains, at other times, it won't. In a sense, he was giving in to his need for adventure. Being impatient, a signature that is typical of the 5 Personal Year, he did not give enough thought to the current downward state of the real estate market.

- When numbers change, be realistic in your expectations. Just because you are moving into an 8 Pinnacle, for example, it does not mean that you will become a financial mogul overnight. If you have no 8s among your numbers, you are typically not motivated by money and business. The 8 Pinnacle might simply bring increased

---

4. A consultation at the end of that 5 Year showed clearly that this was an unfortunate time for financial investments. This information was strongly supported by astrological factors.

opportunities for material rewards, worldly recognition, or success. But it will not necessarily make you a Donald Trump.

- Look for patterns of numbers. The 2 and 6 combination usually indicates periods during which love and relationships are important, while 4s combined with 8s are more focused on business and money. When 3s, 6s, and 9s are found together, the arts and self-expression are important, while 1s and 5s focus on individuality and creativity. The 1s, 5s, and 9s bring the most significant change, while the 2s and 9s bring emotional situations and drama.

The numbers do not change you, and although they may give the general tone, purpose, and direction of your life journey, you remain free to navigate its waters. With the powerful and fascinating knowledge of your numbers, you will now be in a position to make the most appropriate choices given your personal trends.

Bibliography

Campbell, Florence. *Your Days Are Numbered.* Marina del Rey, CA: DeVorss & Company, 2002.

Christel, Alain-Victor. *Le Guide Pratique de la Nouvelle Numérologie.* Paris, France: De Vecchi Poche, 1989.

Cope, Lloyd. *The Astrologer's Forecasting Workbook.* Tempe, AZ: American Federation of Astrologers, Inc., 1995.

Covey, Stephen R. *The 7 Secrets of Highly Effective People.* New York: Fireside, 1990.

Decoz, Hans, and Tom Monte. *Numerology: Key to Your Inner Self.* New York: Perigee, 2002.

Goodwin, Matthew Oliver. *Numerology: The Complete Guide, Volume I.* North Hollywood, CA: Newcastle Publishing Company, 1981.

Goodwin, Matthew Oliver. *Numerology: The Complete Guide, Volume II.* North Hollywood, CA: Newcastle Publishing Company, 1981.

Tapiero, Martal A. O. *Les Nombres et le Destin.* Unpublished edition, 1979.

Index

Free Catalog

Get the latest information on our body, mind, and spirit products! To receive a **free** copy of Llewellyn's consumer catalog, *New Worlds of Mind & Spirit,* simply call 1-877-NEW-WRLD or visit our website at www.llewellyn.com and click on *New Worlds.*

LLEWELLYN ORDERING INFORMATION

Order Online:
Visit our website at www.llewellyn.com, select your books, and order them on our secure server.

Order by Phone:
- Call toll-free within the U.S. at 1-877-NEW-WRLD (1-877-639-9753). Call toll-free within Canada at 1-866-NEW-WRLD (1-866-639-9753)
- We accept VISA, MasterCard, and American Express

Order by Mail:
Send the full price of your order (MN residents add 6.5% sales tax) in U.S. funds, plus postage & handling to:

Llewellyn Worldwide
2143 Wooddale Drive, Dept. 978-0-7387-1149-2
Woodbury, MN 55125-2989

Postage & Handling:
Standard (U.S., Mexico, & Canada). If your order is:
$24.99 and under, add $3.00
$25.00 and over, FREE STANDARD SHIPPING

AK, HI, PR: $15.00 for one book plus $1.00 for each additional book.

International Orders (airmail only):
$16.00 for one book plus $3.00 for each additional book

Orders are processed within 2 business days.
Please allow for normal shipping time. Postage and handling rates subject to change.

Astrological Crosses in Relationships
Understanding Cardinal, Fixed & Mutable Energies

Pauline Edward

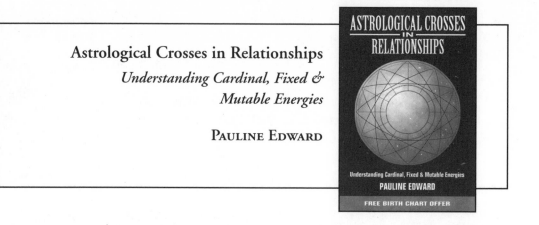

For the first time ever, a book boldly brings to light a previously overlooked, yet crucial, component of chart interpretation. They are the crosses (also known as quadruplicities or modes): the Cardinal, Fixed, and Mutable qualities in the zodiac.

Knowledge of the crosses will help you recognize astrological features by the way someone expresses himself. You will gain a better understanding of what motivates people's decisions and actions. Planetary configurations and transits will take on a whole new meaning. As you include the crosses in your interpretations, you will also be able to predict the success of relationships with uncanny accuracy.

978-0-7387-0199-8
216 pp., 6 x 9 $14.95

To order, call 1-877-NEW-WRLD

Prices subject to change without notice

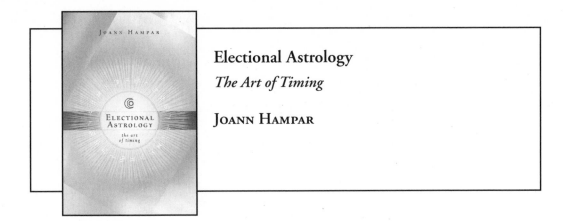

Electional Astrology

The Art of Timing

JOANN HAMPAR

Planning a wedding? Scheduling surgery? Buying a house? How do you choose a date and time that offers the best chance of success? The odds are in your favor when you plan life events using electional astrology—a branch of astrology that helps you align with the power of the universe.

Professional astrologer Joann Hampar teaches the principles of electional astrology—explaining the significance of each planet and how to time events according to their cycles. Readers will learn how to analyze the planetary alignments and compile an electional chart that pinpoints the optimal time to buy a diamond ring, adopt a pet, close a business deal, take a trip, move, file an insurance claim, take an exam, schedule a job interview, and just about anything else!

978-0-7387-0701-3
216 pp., 6 x 9, charts $14.95

To order, call 1-877-NEW-WRLD

Prices subject to change without notice

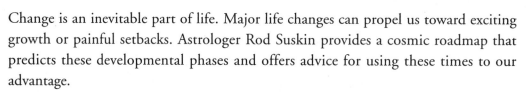

Cycles of Life

Understanding the Principles of
Predictive Astrology

Rod Suskin

Change is an inevitable part of life. Major life changes can propel us toward exciting growth or painful setbacks. Astrologer Rod Suskin provides a cosmic roadmap that predicts these developmental phases and offers advice for using these times to our advantage.

Cycles of Life describes how the planets are implicitly connected to important transitions in our lives. Easy-to-follow tables and worksheets help readers track planetary cycles and interpret the results. From there, individuals can gain a new understanding of the past and begin preparing for future life changes. The author also shares how the planets affect many aspects of life, including relationships, money management, business, and daily living.

978-0-7387-0659-7
264 pp., 6 x 9, tables $16.95

Numerology for Beginners

Easy Guide to Love, Money, Destiny

GERIE BAUER

Every letter and number in civilization has a particular power, or vibration. For centuries, people have read these vibrations through the practice of numerology. References in the Bible even describe Jesus using numerology to change the names of his disciples. *Numerology for Beginners* is a quick ready-to-use reference that lets you find your personal vibrations based on the numbers associated with your birthdate and name.

Within minutes, you will be able to assess the vibrations surrounding a specific year, month, and day—even a specific person. Detect whether you're in a business cycle or a social cycle, and whether a certain someone or occupation would be compatible with you. Plus, learn to detect someone's personality within seconds of learning his/her first name!

978-1-56718-057-2
288 pp., 5³⁄₁₆ x 8 $11.95

To order, call 1-877-NEW-WRLD

Prices subject to change without notice

To Write to the Author

If you wish to contact the author or would like more information about this book, please write to the author in care of Llewellyn Worldwide and we will forward your request. Both the author and publisher appreciate hearing from you and learning of your enjoyment of this book and how it has helped you. Llewellyn Worldwide cannot guarantee that every letter written to the author can be answered, but all will be forwarded. Please write to:

Pauline Edward
℅ Llewellyn Worldwide
2143 Wooddale Drive, Dept. 978-0-7387-1149-2
Woodbury, MN 55125-2989, U.S.A.

Please enclose a self-addressed stamped envelope for reply,
or $1.00 to cover costs. If outside U.S.A., enclose
international postal reply coupon.

Many of Llewellyn's authors have websites with additional information and resources. For more information, please visit our website at:

www.llewellyn.com